MIGRATION RECORDS
A Guide for Family Historians

MIGRATION RECORDS

A Guide for Family Historians

Roger Kershaw

The National Archives

First published in 2009 by
The National Archives
Kew, Richmond
Surrey, TW9 4DU, UK

www.nationalarchives.gov.uk

The National Archives brings together the Public Record
Office, Historical Manuscripts Commission, Office of
Public Sector Information and Her Majesty's Stationery
Office.

A catalogue card for this book is available from the
British Library.

ISBN   978 1 905615 40 7

Design by Peters & Zabransky UK Ltd.
Jacket design by Ken Wilson | point 918

Printed in the UK by TJ International Ltd,
Padstow, Cornwall

COVER IMAGES: (centre) Immigrants arriving at Victoria
Station, London, 27 May 1956 (Photo by Haywood
Magee/Getty Images); (above) Arriving in London
(INF 9/386).
IMAGES IN THE TEXT: Figs 9 and 18 appear courtesy of the
Jewish Museum (*www.jewishmuseum.org*) and the Wok-
ing Muslim Mission (*www.wokingmuslim.org*) respec-
tively. The rest of the images in this book are taken from
the files of the National Archives and, unless otherwise
mentioned, are © Crown Copyright.

Some of the material in this book previously appeared in
Immigrants and Aliens by Roger Kershaw and Mark
Pearsall and *Emigrants and Expats* by Roger Kershaw
(Public Record Office, 2000 and 2002 respectively).

The publishers would like to thank Abi Husainy, Modern
Records Specialist at the National Archives, for permission to quote material in chapter 3.

ACKNOWLEDGEMENTS

I should like to thank the following people at the
National Archives for their assistance with this publica-
tion: Hugh Alexander, Catherine Bradley, Brian Carter,
Paul Johnson, Mark Pearsall and Tom Wharton.

CONTENTS

USING THE NATIONAL ARCHIVES

The National Archives is the national repository for government records in the UK. Its main site at Kew holds the surviving records of government back to the Domesday Book (1086) and beyond.

Most of the records described in this guide can be consulted at the National Archives, Kew, Richmond, Surrey, TW9 4DU. The archives are open 09:00–17:00 on Mondays and Fridays, 09:00–19:00 on Tuesdays and Thursdays, 10:00–17:00 on Wednesdays and 09:30–17:00 on Saturdays. They are closed on Sundays, public holidays and for annual stocktaking. This normally happens on the first full weekend in December. The website address is:

www.nationalarchives.gov.uk

The National Archives is about 10 minutes' walk from Kew Gardens Underground Station, which is on London Transport's District Line, as well as the London Overground Service. For motorists, it is just off the South Circular Road (A205). There is adequate parking.

The National Archives can be a confusing place to use. If you are new to researching there, it is a good idea to allow plenty of time to find your feet. The staff are both knowledgeable and friendly, and are happy to help if you get lost. There is a public restaurant and a well-stocked bookshop on site. Self-service lockers are available to store your belongings.

Accessing the records is simple. First you need to obtain a reader's ticket, which is free, when you arrive. Please bring two forms of identity, such as a passport or driving licence, and something with an address, such as a utility bill or bank statement. If you are not a British citizen, you will need your passport. For further information see:

www.nationalarchives.gov.uk/visit/whattobring.htm

It is possible to get photocopies and/or digital copies of most documents you find: please ask the staff for details. It is also possible for you to use your own digital camera to copy documents.

In order to protect the documents, each one of which is unique, security in the reading rooms is tight. You are only permitted to take a camera, laptop, notebook and notes into the reading rooms, and may only use a pencil. Eating and drinking are not permitted in the reading rooms.

The records held by the National Archives are described and ordered using a three-part reference. The first element is known as the 'department' and takes the form of letters. The 'department' denotes which government department created the records. The second element is known as the 'series' and collects together records of a similar type. The second element is in the form of numbers. The third and final element of a document reference is known as the 'piece' and this usually is just a number, but occasionally may include letters.

Over time, terminology used to describe the document ('piece' is the term used by the National Archives) references at the National Archives has changed, and you may hear terms such as 'letter codes' and 'class' still being used. Letter codes are, of course, the 'department' and 'class' is the 'series'. Whilst such terminology is interchangeable, many of the 'department' identities, irrespective of whether they are being called 'department' or 'letter code', are obvious, with FO being the Foreign Office, MEPO being the Metropolitan Police Office and BT being the Board of Trade. Other 'department' identities are not so obvious; the records of MI5, for example, are identified by the letters KV while the Welsh Office uses BD.

Each piece reference is unique. For example, the department code for Home Office is HO; the series number for the Aliens Department: General Files and Aliens Naturalization and Nationality Files is 213; and the piece number for Nationality: Policy: Jewish Refuges, 1940 is 44. This gives a complete National Archives reference of HO 213/44. These references can be discovered from the various finding aids in The National Archives and via the web using the Catalogue:

www.nationalarchives.gov.uk/catalogue

This contains details of our holdings of nearly 10 million files, organized by creating department. You can search these by title of document and narrow your search by year(s) and department code. You can then order these prior to your visit or request copies to be sent to you by post.

An increasing number of records are available on microfilm, microfiche or in digitized format. Where this is the case, the fact is noted in the text. You do not need to order microfilms on the computer as you can help yourself to them in the Open Reading Room.

In addition, there are various other finding aids for genealogists. The best general overview is provided by Amanda Bevan's revised *Tracing Your Ancestors in The National Archives* (7th edition, TNA, 2006).

The National Archives Online

As well as giving information on where the National Archives is, opening times and how to gain access, the National Archives website gives details about popular records, including research guides and lists of independent researchers. Most importantly, the website allows readers to access the National Archives Catalogue (series lists).

The Catalogue can be searched by using keywords, dates and, if you know them, the department (letter code) and series (class) where records are known to exist.

Follow these simple steps to identify the documents you require:

1 Locate the Catalogue.
2 Click on Search the Catalogue.
3 Type in keyword(s) into the top box, the year range (as appropriate) into the two boxes below the keyword box and, if known, the departmental code and series (optional) into the last (bottom) box.
4 It is possible to use more than one keyword, either by just putting the words in or by doing a combined word search linking the words together with AND.
5 Click on Search.

The computer will then search for documents of interest that include the search term(s) you used and that are included in a document description. Document descriptions and the references under which they will need to be ordered will be listed as either individual items or, in the case of multiple results, under the department code (the letters) and then with the number of results in blue at the right-hand side. Click on the blue number to obtain more detailed descriptions of these results.

Many records have been or are in the process of being digitized and placed on the DocumentsOnline section of the National Archives website. Relevant examples include Alien Registration cards in MEPO 35 and the Southwell Workhouse and Poor Law Union Papers in MH 12. In each case it is possible to search these records by name and, where appropriate, to download them (for a fee).

Records Held Elsewhere

Many records of value for family and local history are held in other record offices and libraries. The National Register of Archives – maintained by the National Archives and available on the National Archives website – contains information about the whereabouts of records in local record offices and local studies libraries and in other repositories in England and Wales. The A2A database contains catalogues describing archives held locally in England and Wales and dating from the eighth century to the present day.

INTRODUCTION

Britain has often been described as a nation of immigrants. Flemish and Huguenot migrants in the 1500s and 1600s were followed by Irish migrants in the 1700s and 1800s and Jewish migrants in the late 1800s. More recently, those who travelled from the colonies and Poland after the Second World War have been joined by, among others, refugees from Kenya and Uganda and migrants from within the European Union. However, during the same period, it has been estimated that more than 17 million persons have emigrated from the British Isles.

There are always reasons why people move from one place to another and these are often described as 'pull' and 'push' factors. The 'push' factor is more often the case when a decision to migrate has been enforced. 'Push' reasons to migrate voluntarily include the need to seek political or religious freedom or the need to escape war or poverty. 'Push' enforced migration relates mainly to transportation – a period of exile overseas in British territory during which a convict would be forced to work productively and learn new habits of industry while at the same time benefit the development of the colonial economy.

The 'pull' factor is less prominent. This is when people have been lured to migrate for economic reasons. For example, the Land and Emigration Commission actively fostered emigration to the Colonies and Dominions by offering free passages and free land grants.

The purpose of this guide is to help researchers appreciate and understand the wide variety of records concerning migrants held at the National Archives, at other archives and (increasingly) online. Its intended audience is family historians seeking information relating to their own ancestry, but it is also for the use of social and economic historians interested in the history of immigration, patterns of migration, and its impact on British society over the past eight hundred years.

Migration Records offers guidance to what the records contain and suggestions on how they might be used. It explores the movement of people into, out of and within Britain, as well as tracing migration policy and how it has evolved over the centuries. *Migration Records* also discusses those government departments responsible for controlling the movement of people, and explains why certain records were preserved as archives and others were not. It is of course impossible to cover everything, but the book does not restrict itself to sources at the

National Archives. Records of migrants are scattered across archives in the United Kingdom and overseas as there is not a dedicated archive for immigration or emigration within the United Kingdom.

Having said this, the National Archives has one of the largest collections of material related to migrants. Its holdings – over 10 million items from central government, courts of law and other UK national bodies – can be searched on its online catalogue *www.nationalarchives.gov.uk/catalogue*. Its website also provides details of opening hours, an increasing range of online records and exhibitions and a link to the Moving Here site *www.movinghere.org.uk,* which is dedicated to exploring, recording and illustrating why people came to England over the last 200 years. It offers free access, for personal and educational use, to an online catalogue of versions of original material related to migration history from local, regional and national archives, libraries and museums.

The structure of the book allows the user to concentrate on specific key migration themes, such as those records associated with the physical arrival or departure of people (chapter 1), or those relating to citizenship (chapter 6). There is also a thematic or subject arrangement looking at specific groups or categories of migrants in the medieval, early modern and modern eras, supported by a number of case studies. A more detailed index at the back of the book allows researchers to dip into the guide at leisure.

Some of the terminology will appear to be strange today, but it is essential to use such terms when carrying out any detailed research at the National Archives. Where you would expect to search using words like immigrants and foreigners you may instead find yourself researching terms such as strangers and aliens, reflecting the perspective of a different age.

These records can prove extremely rich in content, however you choose to approach them. Some, such as naturalization records, can be particularly revealing. These documents, produced as their subject sought to become a naturalized British subject, provide details of not only the subject, but also of their spouse, children, and parents, as well as addresses, occupations, status in the community and country of origin. Others, such as the failed appeals and petitions of those transported to Australia, can be equally detailed, but deeply tragic. Together they can help to piece together the story behind your ancestors' decision to leave or come to these shores, and the life they found when they did.

1 ARRIVING AND DEPARTING

If you are trying to find details of someone who migrated to or from the British Isles, the best place to start is in the sources recording the preparation for departure or the actual departure itself. Such records will include visas, passports, certificates of arrival, travel permits, and passenger lists. Survival of these records is, however, rather patchy and depends much on the legislation in force at the time of creation. This will inevitably vary from one country to another, but a general rule of thumb is that sources recording migrants entering a country are normally much more detailed than those recording migrants leaving.

In overall terms it must be said that the increasing online presence of these records means that it is far easier to research them than it used to be. Many of these original sources, located in archives across the globe, can now be accessed in the comfort of your living room.

1.1 Sources on Entry to the UK

1.1.1 Aliens' Certificates of Arrival, 1793–1905

In 1793 an Act (33 Geo. III c. IV) was passed 'respecting Aliens arriving in this Kingdom, or resident therein, in certain cases'. Great Britain was then at war with France as part of the First Coalition, and the Act was extended by subsequent Acts until the end of the Napoleonic Wars. Together these Acts established a system for regulating so-called 'aliens'.

Non-British citizens arriving in British ports were required by the Acts to sign a declaration that would then be certified into the Home Office by customs officers or local agents. New and recent arrivals had to give their names, ranks, occupations and addresses to a local Justice of the Peace (JP). Householders who took in an alien as a lodger had to deliver similar details to the overseer of the parish, and returns and samples of these 'Accounts of Aliens' and 'Householders' Notices and Overseers' Returns' were sent to the Clerk of the Peace so that he could lay them before Quarter Sessions. A smattering of material from these lists can be found among returns of Quarter Sessions at local archives. For example, there are 38 accounts of aliens from eight Middlesex parishes in 1797 and 10 householders' notices from five parishes in 1798 included in Quarter Session records at the London Metropolitan Archives.

Although the Acts and the powers they conveyed had been conceived as wartime measures such regulations were here to stay. Further legislation would follow whose focus was on the potential dangers of foreign 'criminal and hostile persons' resident in the country. The net result, whatever the underlying rationale, is that those of us with foreign ancestors who moved to Britain are increasingly likely to be able to find evidence of their arrival from this point onwards.

The Act passed in 1816 (56 Geo. III c. 86) was key to this. The Act required masters of vessels to declare in writing to the Inspector of Aliens or Officer of the Customs the number of aliens on board, specifying their names and descriptions, and the aliens themselves were required to make a similar declaration. Each new arrival was to be issued with a certificate, showing the ship's name, and his or her own name, description, place of departure, destination and profession, with space for references and remarks. Unless he or she was a servant, the alien was to produce the certificate within one week to a magistrate or a JP, and copies of the entries on the certificates were to be sent both by the port and by the magistrate or JP to the Secretary of State in London. The Act applied to all aliens except seamen, ambassadors and their domestic servants, and children under 14. Most of these provisions had previously been included in the 1793 Act, but this new Act made the first provision for any central system of registration, which was applied to foreign nationals already resident in the British Isles.

Further innovation was introduced in 1826 when the new 'Act for the Registration of Aliens' was passed (7 Geo. IV c. 46). From 1 July of that year every alien was expected to make a declaration 'of his name, abode, etc.; and transmit the same within fourteen days to the Aliens

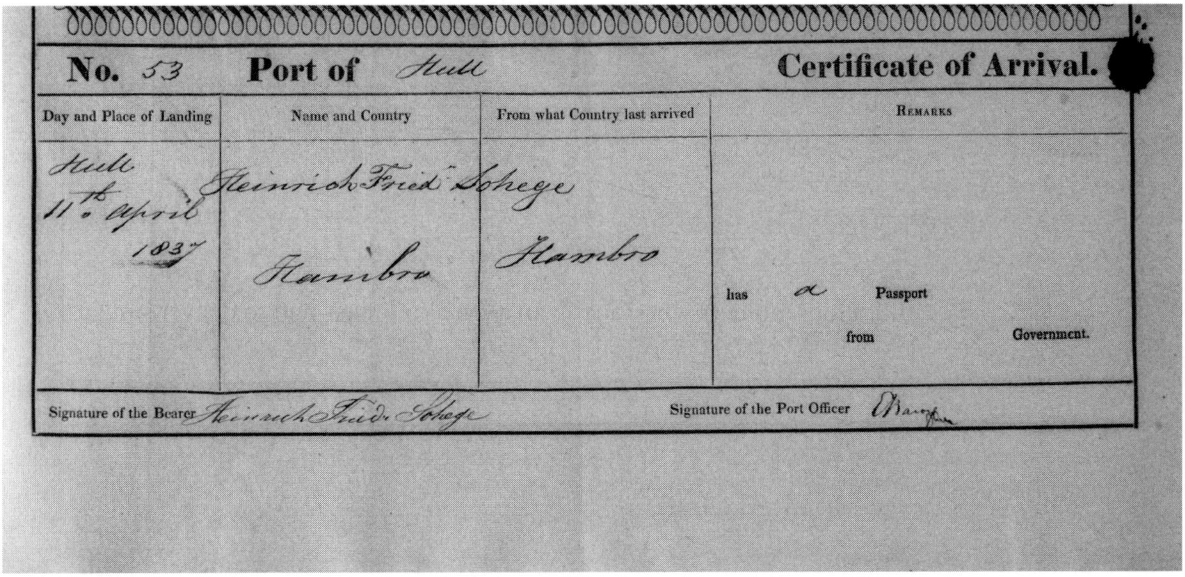

FIG. 1 *Certificate of arrival for Heinrich Fried Sohege.*
HO 2/20

No. 53	Port of Hull		Certificate of Arrival.
Day and Place of Landing	Name and Country	From what Country last arrived	REMARKS
Hull 11th April 1837	Heinrich Fried. Sohege Hambro	Hambro	has a Passport from Government.
Signature of the Bearer Heinrich Fried. Sohege		Signature of the Port Officer	

Office in Great Britain, or to the chief secretary for Ireland'. This had to be done every six months. On receipt of the declaration, the clerk at the Aliens Office would send a certificate similar to that described in the 1816 Act. Aliens were also required to make a declaration before leaving the country and, for the first time, they were required to produce police registration certificates. Added to the list of exemptions were those resident in the country for more than seven years.

The Act (7 Will. IV c. II) passed in 1836 repealed that of 1826; it introduced some relaxation in the system of registration, but continued the requirement that masters of vessels and aliens should make a declaration on arrival. Certificates were still issued and copies sent to the Secretary of State in London. Similarly, police registration certificates still had to be produced, although it was no longer necessary to visit or send a written declaration to the Aliens Office, and the declaration they made on leaving the country was in future to be made at the Customs Office at the port of departure. An alien living in this country was no longer required to report his or her address every six months, and was in future to become exempt from the provisions of the Act after three years instead of seven.

Most of the early records of the Aliens Office have been destroyed, but FO 83/21–2 contains lists of aliens arriving at British ports for the period August 1810–May 1811. No certificates of arrival of aliens survive for the period 1816–25. Certificates issued under the Aliens Act 1826 were destroyed, when the Aliens Office was absorbed into the Home Office in 1836.

HO 5/25–32 contains an index of certificates from 1826 to 1849, and CUST 102/393–6 contains Board of Customs copies of certificates of arrivals at the port of Gravesend for the years 1826–37. See HO 2 for original certificates of arrival of individual aliens arranged under ports of arrival for the period 1836–52. Each gives name, nationality, profession, date of arrival and last country visited, with a signature, and occasionally other particulars (Fig. 1). The Treasury agreed to a proposal in 1849 by Sir George Grey, the Secretary of State for the Home Department, to abolish the register, and no certificates survive after 1852.

All of the surviving records described above (and HO 3 described below) have been digitized by Ancestry (*www.ancestry.co.uk*) in association with the National Archives and can be searched and downloaded through either website from spring 2009. Both series can be searched by name, nationality, port of departure, date of arrival and port of arrival.

1.1.2   *Aliens' passenger lists, 1836–1905*

Returns of alien passengers made by masters of ships under s.2 of the Act of 1836 can be found in HO 3. As with HO 2 the lists do not extend beyond the mid-part of the nineteenth century, surviving for the period July 1836 to January 1861 and December 1866 to December 1869. From this point onwards, the Home Office preserved the lists for only

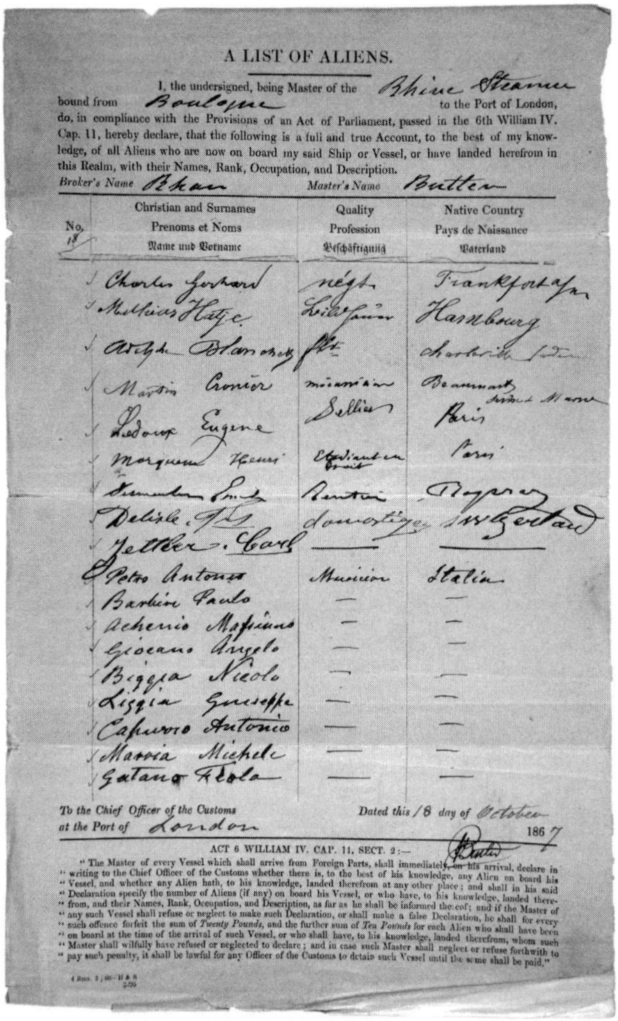

A LIST OF ALIENS.

I, the undersigned, being Master of the Rhine Steamer bound from Boulogne to the Port of London, do, in compliance with the Provisions of an Act of Parliament, passed in the 6th William IV. Cap. 11, hereby declare, that the following is a full and true Account, to the best of my knowledge, of all Aliens who are now on board my said Ship or Vessel, or have landed herefrom in this Realm, with their Names, Rank, Occupation, and Description.

Broker's Name [illegible] *Master's Name* Butler

No. 18	Christian and Surnames / Prenoms et Noms / Name und Vorname	Quality / Profession / Beschäftigung	Native Country / Pays de Naissance / Vaterland
	Charles Gerhard	négt.	Frankfort a/m
	Mathias Hatje	[illegible]	Hambourg
	Adolphe [illegible]	[illegible]	Charleville [illegible]
	Martin Cronier	[illegible]	Beaumont [illegible]
	Ledoux Eugene	Sellier	Paris
	Marquem Henri	[illegible]	Paris
	[illegible]	[illegible]	[illegible]
	Delisle [illegible]	domestique	Switzerland
	Jetter Carl	—	—
	Petro Antonio	Musician	Italia
	Barbiri Paolo	—	—
	Acherio [illegible]	—	—
	Giocano Angelo	—	—
	Biggia Nicolo	—	—
	Liggia Giuseppe	—	—
	Capurro Antonio	—	—
	Marria Michele	—	—
	Gatano [illegible]	—	—

To the Chief Officer of the Customs at the Port of London *Dated this* 18 *day of* October 1867

Butler

ACT 6 WILLIAM IV. CAP. 11. SECT. 2:—

"The Master of every Vessel which shall arrive from Foreign Parts, shall immediately, on his arrival, declare in "writing to the Chief Officer of the Customs whether there is, to the best of his knowledge, any Alien on board his "Vessel, and whether any Alien hath, to his knowledge, landed therefrom at any other place; and shall in his said "Declaration specify the number of Aliens (if any) on board his Vessel, or who have, to his knowledge, landed there- "from, and their Names, Rank, Occupation, and Description, as far as he shall be informed thereof; and if the Master of "any such Vessel shall refuse or neglect to make such Declaration, or shall make a false Declaration, he shall for every "such offence forfeit the sum of *Twenty Pounds*, and the further sum of *Ten Pounds* for each Alien who shall have been "on board at the time of the arrival of such Vessel, or who shall have, to his knowledge, landed therefrom, whom such "Master shall wilfully have refused or neglected to declare; and in case such Master shall neglect or refuse forthwith to "pay such penalty, it shall be lawful for any Officer of the Customs to detain such Vessel until the same shall be paid."

FIG. 2 *A list of aliens, including nine Italian musicians, travelling to London from Boulogne in October 1867.*
HO 3/102

five years after which they were destroyed under statute. The lists are arranged chronologically and there are four per year.

Later lists do not survive, largely because they were seen at the time as unreliable and incomplete. In the minutes of evidence taken before the Select Committee on Laws affecting Aliens in 1843 (Parliamentary Papers reference 1843, volume V, page 145), it was reported that no lists were provided by the masters at Liverpool in 1842 and there was no registration of aliens; at other ports the masters' lists showed that many aliens landed but failed to register. At London, 7,716 landed and 4,493 registered; at Dover, 1,277 landed and 1,237 registered; at Southampton, 1,197 landed and none registered; at Hull, 794 landed and one registered. In all, 11,600 aliens landed and 6,084 registered. In theory, the penalty for an alien failing to register was £2, and for a master failing to provide a list £20, but it appears that these fines were never exacted.

1.1.3 *Board of Trade incoming passenger lists, 1878–1960*

Patchy survival of records is unlikely to be a problem if you are researching ancestors and relatives who arrived in this country after 1878. In association with Ancestry, the National Archives has digitized the incoming passenger lists in the series BT 26, covering the period 1878–1960. The 1,500 boxes of lists in this series record the voyages of some 16 million people who arrived at British ports between 1878 and 1960. This site can be searched by name of passenger, birth date or age, arrival date, port of departure, port of arrival, ports of voyage, if recorded, vessel name, shipping line, ship's official number, and original source reference.

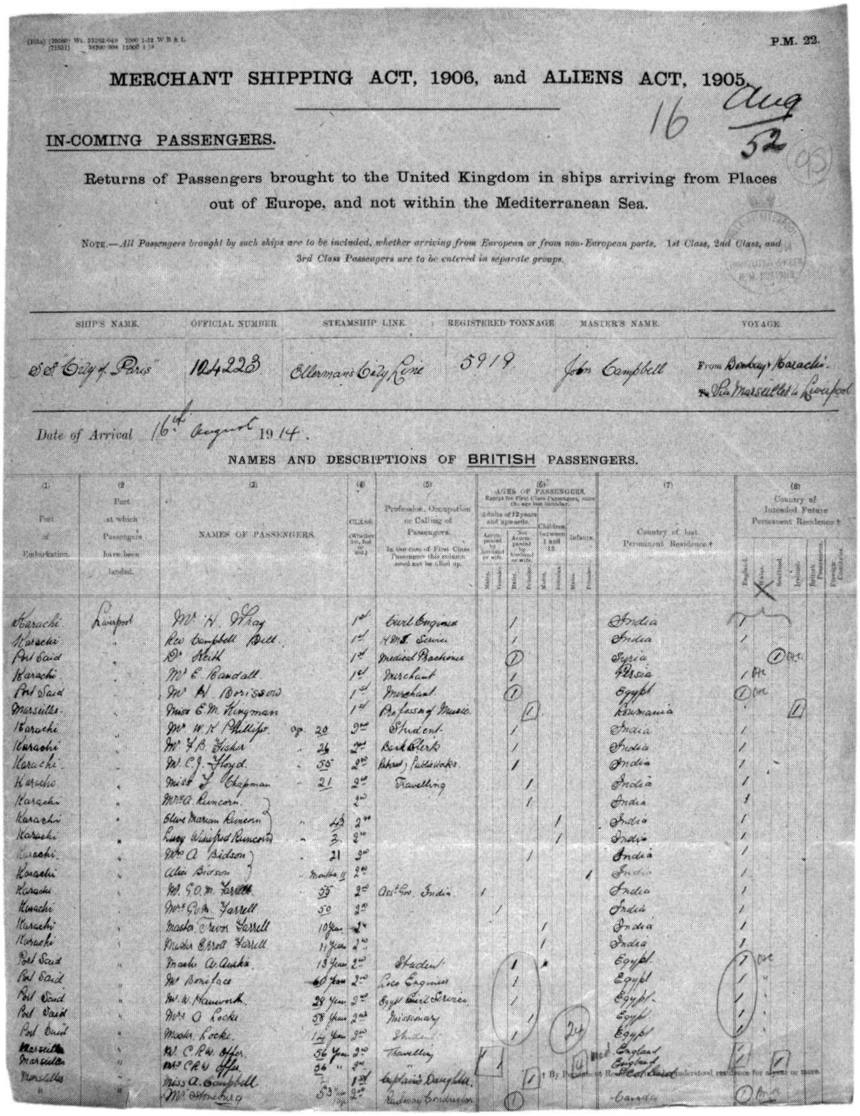

P.M. 22.

MERCHANT SHIPPING ACT, 1906, and ALIENS ACT, 1905.

16 Aug 52

IN-COMING PASSENGERS.

Returns of Passengers brought to the United Kingdom in ships arriving from Places out of Europe, and not within the Mediterranean Sea.

NOTE.—*All Passengers brought by such ships are to be included, whether arriving from European or from non-European ports. 1st Class, 2nd Class, and 3rd Class Passengers are to be entered in separate groups.*

SHIP'S NAME.	OFFICIAL NUMBER.	STEAMSHIP LINE.	REGISTERED TONNAGE.	MASTER'S NAME.	VOYAGE.
S.S. City of Paris	124223	Ellerman's City Line	5919	John Campbell	From Bombay, Karachi via Marseilles to Liverpool

Date of Arrival 16th August 1914.

NAMES AND DESCRIPTIONS OF BRITISH PASSENGERS.

(1) Port of Embarkation.	(2) Port at which Passengers have been landed.	(3) NAMES OF PASSENGERS.	Age	(4) CLASS.	(5) Profession, Occupation or Calling of Passengers.	(7) Country of last Permanent Residence.†
Karachi	Liverpool	Mr H. Wray		1st	Civil Engineer	India
Karachi	"	Rev Campbell Bell		1st	H.M.S. Service	India
Port Said	"	Dr Keith		1st	Medical Practioner	Syria
Karachi	"	Mr E. Randall		1st	Merchant	Persia
Port Said	"	Mr H. Borissow		1st	Merchant	Egypt
Marseilles	"	Miss E.M. Kingman		1st	Professor of Music	Roumania
Karachi	"	Mr W.K. Phillips	20	2nd	Student	India
Karachi	"	Mr F.B. Fisher	26	2nd	Bank Clerk	India
Karachi	"	Mr C.J. Floyd	55	2nd	Retired, Public Works	India
Karachi	"	Miss L. Chapman	21	2nd	Travelling	India
Karachi	"	Mrs A. Runcorn		2nd		India
Karachi	"	Olive Marian Runcorn	43	2nd		India
Karachi	"	Lucy Winifred Runcorn	3	2nd		India
Karachi	"	Mrs A. Bidson	21	2nd		India
Karachi	"	Alice Bidson	months 11	2nd		India
Karachi	"	Mr G.O.M. Farrell	55	2nd	Asst Gov. India	India
Karachi	"	Mrs G.O.M. Farrell	50	2nd		India
Karachi	"	Master Trevor Farrell	10 years	2nd		India
Karachi	"	Master Errol Farrell	11 years	2nd		India
Port Said	"	Master A. Austin	13 years	2nd	Student	Egypt
Port Said	"	Mr Boniface	60 years	2nd	Loco Engineer	Egypt
Port Said	"	Mr W. Haworth	28 years	2nd	Egypt Civil Service	Egypt
Port Said	"	Mrs O. Locke	58 years	2nd	Missionary	Egypt
Port Said	"	Master Locke	14 years	2nd	Student	Egypt
Marseilles	"	Mr C.R.W. Offer	56 years	2nd	Travelling	England
Marseilles	"	Mrs C.R.W. Offer	56 "	2nd	"	England
Marseilles	"	Miss A. Campbell		1st	Captain's Daughter	Scotland
"	"	Mr Honeburg	53 years	2nd	Railway Contractor	Canada

† By Permanent Residence is to be understood residence for a year or more.

FIG. 3 *Passengers arriving from Bombay in the first weeks of the First World War.* BT 26/581

The original records were created by the Board of Trade, copies of which were also kept by the numerous shipping companies ferrying people to and from Britain over the centuries. The collection starts in 1878 (note that ships entering the ports of Queenstown and Liverpool are only included for selected years until 1890) and finishes in 1960, by which time air travel became the preferred method of travel for long haul destinations. Unlike national archives in other countries, the National Archives has never selected air lists for permanent preservation.

The lists selected for preservation exclude those for vessels whose port of departure was within Europe or the Mediterranean area; there are no lists for voyages that began in Ireland and finished in England or began in Calais and ended in London. Ports within Europe will only be included if they were embarkation points for a vessel whose journey had begun outside Europe and the Mediterranean area (e.g. Gibraltar).

The information provided on the list varies depending on when your ancestor travelled. The early lists from 1890 through to about 1910 used pre-printed forms recording information relating to name and occupation and an indication of whether the passenger was male or female, was English, Scottish, Irish or foreign, their age (though in most cases this is not recorded until the turn of the century), and the name of the port at which they were contracted to land. From 1918 a separate age field is recorded and from 1922 a field recording the last address in the UK appears. From the 1950s the lists indicate whether the passenger is intending to stay for less than 12 months and if so for what reason – leisure or business.

The collection includes passenger lists for ships that finished their journeys at Irish ports (for the Republic until 1922 only).

1.2 Sources on Departure from the UK

1.2.1 Passports

Many people are surprised to learn that passports were not made compulsory for people arriving at or leaving from British ports until 1915. Introduced as a wartime measure, it was hoped that they would help prevent any enemy aliens from entering the country. Of particular concern were German spies, large numbers of whom were (quite wrongly) believed to have already made their way into Britain.

A small selection of papers for various types of applications, passports, visas and certificates can be found in the series FO 737/1–130. This series covers the period 1916–83, later pieces being sample forms only. It can be searched by name of applicant, occupation, and place and date of birth. All include a photograph. This was a requirement from 1915 onwards, when the first modern passport was issued after the enactment of the 1914 British Nationality and Status of Aliens Act (4 and 5 Geo. V c.17). Some include details of accompanying children.

These records are very rich in family detail, recording full name, address, date and place of birth, occupation and a physical description. They also include details of referees and details of their intended use of the passport.

Passports did, of course, exist before the First World War and although they were not compulsory over half a million were issued, mainly to diplomats and merchants, between 1795 and 1916 (between 1916 and 1948 a further six million were issued).

British passports were written in Latin or English before 1771, in French between 1772 and 1858 and in English from then onwards. French translations were added for certain sections from 1921. During the eighteenth and nineteenth centuries, passports were issued more frequently, although it was only in the mid-nineteenth century that regulations relating to applications for passports were first formulated. Prior to 1858 passports could be issued to people of all nationalities, whereas from 1858 UK passports became available to UK nationals only. These were issued for a single journey and could be used for any subsequent journey only if countersigned afresh by the ministers or consuls of the countries that the holder intended to visit. Possession of a passport, however, was confined largely to merchants and diplomats, and the vast majority of those travelling overseas had no formal document.

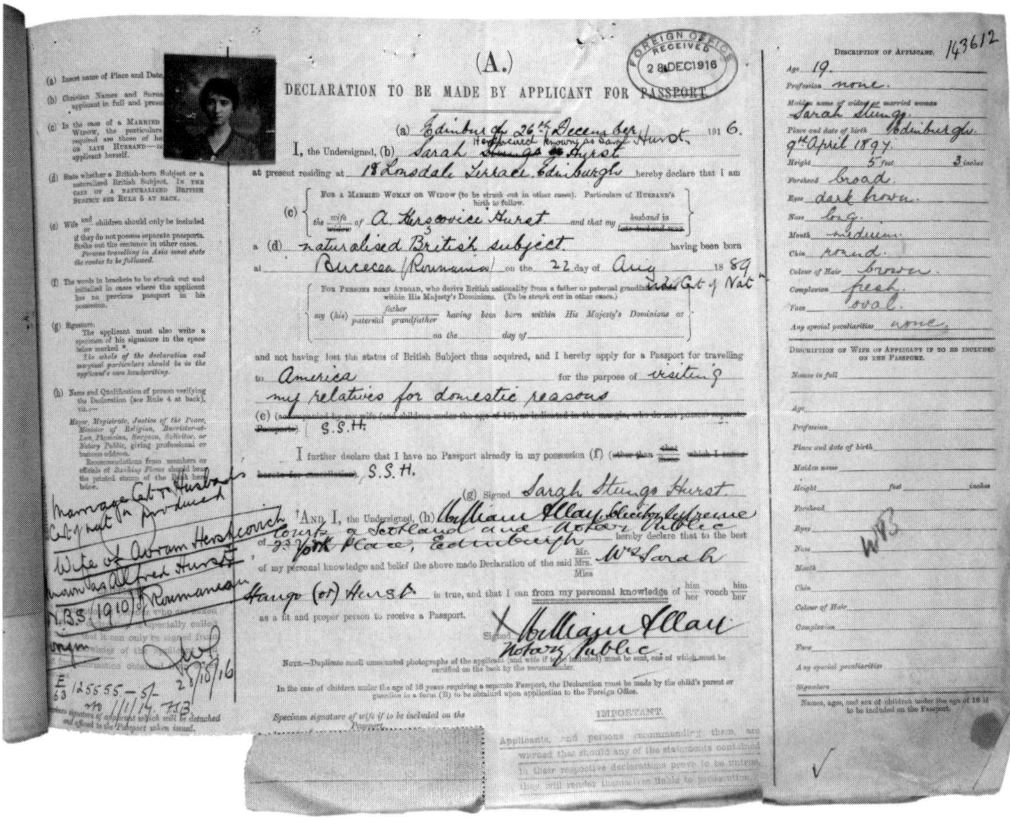
(A.)

DECLARATION TO BE MADE BY APPLICANT FOR PASSPORT

FOREIGN OFFICE RECEIVED 28 DEC 1916

(a) Edinburgh 26th December 1916.

I, the Undersigned, (b) Sarah Stungo Hurst

at present residing at 18 Lonsdale Terrace, Edinburgh hereby declare that I am

(c) FOR A MARRIED WOMAN OR WIDOW (to be struck out in other cases). Particulars of HUSBAND'S birth to follow. the wife of A. Hersovice Hurst and that my husband is

a (d) naturalised British subject having been born at Bucecea (Roumania) on the 22 day of Aug 1889

FOR PERSONS BORN ABROAD, who derive British nationality from a father or paternal grandfather within His Majesty's Dominions. (To be struck out in other cases.) my (his) father / paternal grandfather having been born within His Majesty's Dominions at ___ on the ___ day of ___

and not having lost the status of British Subject thus acquired, and I hereby apply for a Passport for travelling to America for the purpose of visiting my relatives for domestic reasons

(e) S.S.H.

I further declare that I have no Passport already in my possession (f) S.S.H.

(g) Signed Sarah Stungo Hurst.

AND I, the Undersigned, (h) William Allan, Solicitor of Supreme Courts of Scotland and Notary Public of 23 York Place, Edinburgh hereby declare that to the best of my personal knowledge and belief the above made Declaration of the said Mrs. Sarah Stungo (or) Hurst is true, and that I can from my personal knowledge of her vouch for her as a fit and proper person to receive a Passport.

Signed William Allan Notary Public

NOTE.—Duplicate small unmounted photographs of the applicant (and wife if to be included) must be sent, one of which must be certified on the back by the recommender.

In the case of children under the age of 16 years requiring a separate Passport, the Declaration must be made by the child's parent or guardian in a form (B) to be obtained upon application to the Foreign Office.

Specimen signature of wife if to be included on the Passport.

IMPORTANT.

Applicants, and persons recommending them, are warned that should any of the statements contained in their respective declarations prove to be untrue, they will render themselves liable to prosecution.

DESCRIPTION OF APPLICANT. 143612

Age 19.

Profession none.

Maiden name of widow or married woman Sarah Stungo.

Place and date of birth Edinburgh 9th April 1897.

Height 5 feet 3 inches

Forehead broad.

Eyes dark brown.

Nose big.

Mouth medium.

Chin round.

Colour of Hair brown.

Complexion fresh.

Face oval.

Any special peculiarities none.

DESCRIPTION OF WIFE OF APPLICANT IF TO BE INCLUDED ON THE PASSPORT.

Names in full; Age; Profession; Place and date of birth; Maiden name; Height ___ feet ___ inches; Forehead; Eyes; Nose; Mouth; Chin; Colour of Hair; Complexion; Face; Any special peculiarities; Signature

Names, ages, and sex of children under the age of 16 if to be included on the Passport.

FIG. 4 *Sarah Hurst's passport application, December 1916.* FO 737/24/11

From 1915 until 1923 UK passports were valid for two years, but could be renewed for a further four two-year periods. From 1924 until 1967 passports were issued for five years with a renewal period of five years. The standard 10-year passports were introduced in 1968.

Registers of passports issued can be found in the series of records FO 610. The entries are chronological from 1795 to 1948, with a new numerical series starting on the appointment of each new Foreign Secretary, giving 25 separate series of numbers issued to be found here. If you don't know the passport number or when it was issued, there are nominal indexes in FO 611, but these only cover the period 1851–1916, with the exclusion of those for 1856 and 1863 to 1873. The indexes contain the names of passport holders, giving the serial number and date of issue of each passport, allowing easy access to FO 610.

Findmypast have digitized FO 610 for the years 1851–6, 1858–62 and 1874–1903 and the indexes can be searched (for a fee) on their website by name of passport holder. It has to be said, however, that neither the passport indexes in FO 611 nor the registers in FO 610 offer much for the family historian. Aside from full name, passport number and date of issue, there is also sometimes reference to intended destinations, but this is often broadened to name of continent and not country or city.

Applications to certain destinations are grouped together. It is worth consulting the relevant series if you know your ancestor's destination. Registers of passports acquired for travel to Peking, China, in the period 1874–1926, can be found in FO 563 and FO 564; to Germany, 1850–81 in FO 155; to Hanover, 1857–66, in FO 159/28 and 56; to Saxony, 1819–75, in FO 218; to Sicily and Naples, Italy, 1811–60, in FO 166; to Mexico, 1816–1927, in FO 207; to Warsaw, Poland, 1830–1914, in FO 394, and to Barcelona, Spain, 1775–1922, in FO 639. These are arranged chronologically by date of issue.

A highly miscellaneous sample of some 2,000 passports is kept in FO 655. It includes some passports issued in the early nineteenth century by foreign missions in Great Britain to British subjects wishing to travel abroad. This practice ceased in 1858. There is also a large selection of passports issued from British embassies, consulates and high commissions. In addition, there are some foreign passports which, for some reason or another (usually cases of dual nationality), have ended up in the hands of the Passport Office. The passports can be searched by name of passport holder and by date and place of birth if provided.

Passports are not restricted just to Foreign Office records at the National Archives. Until the seventeenth century, the monarch had the prerogative right to control the movement of his subjects overseas, and records of applications for and grants of permission to leave the kingdom are to be found among the records of Chancery (C) and the Exchequer (E). The Colonial Office was responsible for issuing passports to people going to the colonies.

CO 323 Colonies General includes applications for passports to the colonies, 1796–1818, in CO 323/97–116. For the period 1818–1916, when responsibility for passports to all destinations passed to the Foreign Office, applications for passports to the colonies are bound with the ordinary correspondence series for the relevant colony.

The Identity and Passport Services of the Home Office at *www.ips.gov.uk/passport* provides further information about the history of passports and holds some later records. There are also a number of published works that can be consulted on the history of passports, including *The Passport* (2003) by Martin Lloyd.

1.2.2 Licences to pass beyond the seas

Some of the earliest types of passport records at the National Archives are the Licences To Pass Beyond The Seas preserved in the series E 157. These records fall into two main categories: soldiers taking the statutory oath of allegiance under the Act of 1609 before going to serve in the Low Countries between 1613 and 1633 and licences issued to persons going to Europe, chiefly to Holland but also Scotland and Ireland, in the period 1573–1677. From 1610, all people over the age of 18 travelling abroad had to take an oath of allegiance, according to the statute 7 James I c. 6. From 1637 you could not go to the American colonies without a licence from the Commissioners for Plantations.

There are also several registers of passengers to New England, Barbados and other colonies between 1634 and 1639, and one solitary register for 1677. The entries in the registers generally include date, name and destination. Age and place of residence are sometimes also recorded. These particular registers have been printed in J.C. Hotten, *Original Lists of Persons Emigrating to America, 1600–1700* (1874), P.W. Coldham, *The Complete Book of Emigrants, 1607–1776* (1987–93) and P.W. Filby and M.K. Meyer (eds), *Passenger and Immigration Lists Index* (1981 and annual supplements), available to consult at the National Archives. Rather surprisingly, the series includes odd registers of passengers leaving Chester and Liverpool for Ireland in 1632–3 and leaving Gravesend for Barbados, Virginia, Maryland, Holland and Scotland in 1677 (E 157/17, 24 and 31).

1.2.3 Passes and warrants

The series of records SP 25 includes passes and warrants to go abroad. SP 25/111–16 in particular consists of passes, mainly for Europe for 1650–60. A further entry book of passes covering the period 1748–94 is in FO 366/544. Earlier entries usually give an abstract or copy of the pass, but from January 1793 there is merely a name and a date. There is no name index.

SP 44 State Papers: Entry Books: Warrants and Passes 1661–1828 includes, in SP 44/386–413, passes for aliens going abroad and for merchants to trade overseas, giving details such as name of ship, burden, master, cargo, ports of departure and destination, and period of validity,

1697–1784. The records are indexed to 1722 and described in *Calendar of Home Office Papers in the reign of George III, 1760–75*, available in the Map and Large Document Room. These passes were issued to prevent the return from the Continent of persons under attainder for the plot against William III in 1696.

1.2.4 *Board of Trade outgoing passenger lists, 1890–1960*

Those looking for later travellers are likely to find the website *www.ancestorsonboard.com* very useful. Set up in 2007 by findmypast in association with the National Archives, this site is the result of a project to digitize the outgoing ships' passenger lists in BT 27. These records cover some 24 million passengers who endured long-haul voyages made between 1890 and 1960.

The original records in BT 27 were created by the Board of Trade and copies were also kept by the shipping companies. The collection starts in 1890 and, as with the incoming passenger lists in BT 26 (see 1.1.3), finishes in 1960, by which time air travel had taken precedence over long-haul journeys. As noted above, air lists had not been chosen

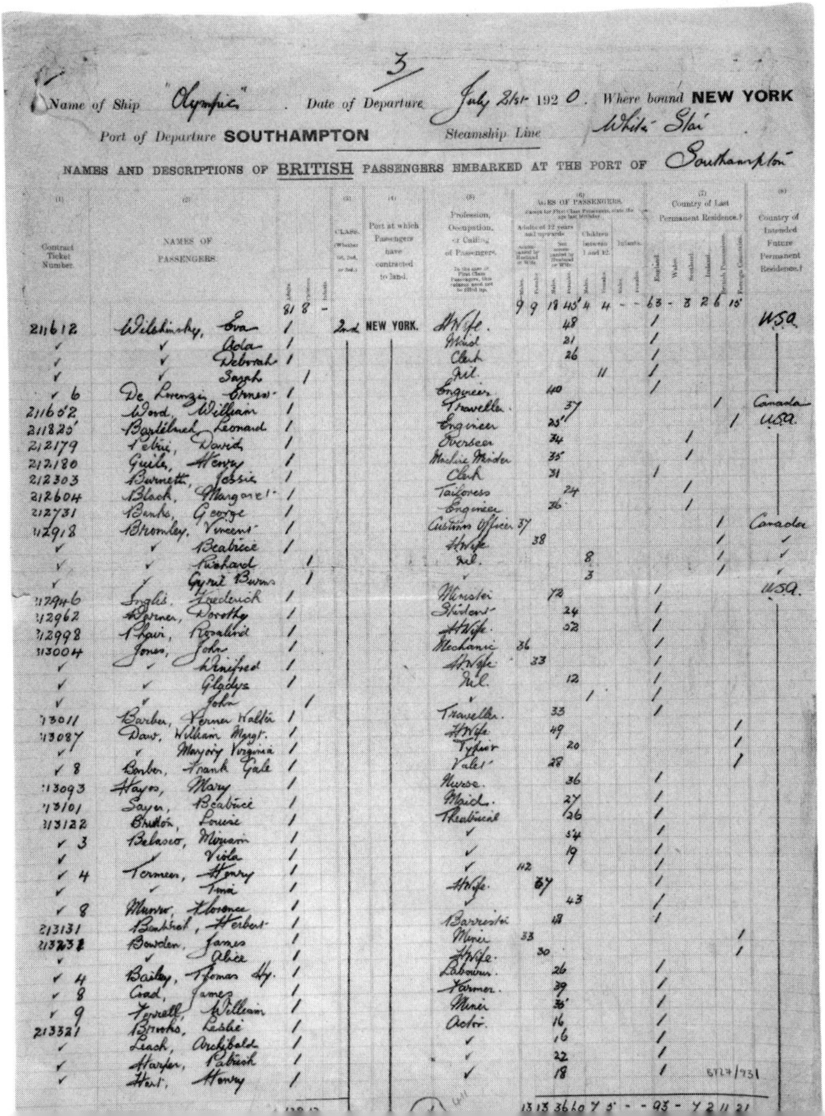
Name of Ship "Olympic" Date of Departure July 21st 1920 Where bound NEW YORK
Port of Departure SOUTHAMPTON Steamship Line White Star
NAMES AND DESCRIPTIONS OF BRITISH PASSENGERS EMBARKED AT THE PORT OF Southampton

FIG. 5 *Outgoing passenger list including Archibald Leach, who later found fame under the stage name Cary Grant.* BT 27/931 for permanent preservation in the National Archives, although some other countries have done so. Again, as with BT 26, the lists selected for preservation exclude those for vessels whose final destination did not extend beyond Europe or the Mediterranean area, so there are no lists for voyages from mainland Britain to Ireland or to France or Spain, unless the journeys continued to a final destination beyond Europe.

The collection can be searched by passenger name on *www.ancestors onboard.com* and individual records viewed. You can narrow down your search by date, gender, port of departure, and country and port of destination if you need to. Information depends on when your ancestor travelled. The early lists from 1890 through to about 1910 used preprinted forms recording information relating to name and occupation, together with an indication of whether the passenger was male or female. Nationality (English, Scottish, Irish or foreign), age (in most cases this is not recorded until the turn of the century), and the name of the port at which they were contracted to land can also be found. From 1918 a separate age field is recorded and from 1922 a field recording the last address in the UK appears. From the 1930s the lists indicate whether the passenger is travelling for the purpose of leisure or tourism and from 1958 exact dates of births are entered on the forms.

The collection includes passenger lists for ships that began their journeys at Irish ports (for the Republic until 1922 only) or began in British ports and picked up passengers at Irish ports (until 1960).

Unfortunately, passenger lists in the custody of the National Archives that predate those on *www.ancestorsonboard.com* are rather scarce and scattered.

1.3 Outgoing Passengers Recorded before 1890

1.3.1 *Port Books*

The earliest examples of passenger lists (though of doubtful use to family historians) can be found in E 190 Exchequer: King's Remembrancer: Port Books 1565–1798. These were compiled as a result of an Exchequer Order of November 1564 requiring all customs officials in the various ports of England and Wales to make their entries in blank books issued by the Exchequer.

Each entry in a Port Book generally contains the name of the ship and its master, the names of the merchants, a description of their goods, and, in the entry books of the collectors, the amount of duties paid. After 1600 most books contain details of the places to and from which shipments were made. However, while some of the exporters were also undoubtedly themselves emigrants, there is no way of distinguishing between the two from the records. The records are not indexed by name though they have been used to compile many of the sources indicated in the bibliography. The records are arranged by port and then by date. The ports named are those that were prosperous and prominent in early modern England and each 'headport', such as Chester, also subsumes a number of (at that time) lesser ports, such as Liverpool and Lancaster.

1.3.2 Colonial Office sources

Those interested in early emigrants to America should see CO 1 Privy Council and related bodies: America and West Indies, Colonial Papers (General Series). This contains lists of passengers, with names and ages, who embarked for the colonies in the 1630s. CO 1/8, ff. 100–02, displays names of passengers bound for New England on board the *Francis of Ipswich* in 1634, while CO 1/9, ff. 246–7, includes names of passengers intended for New England on the *Confidence* in 1636–8.

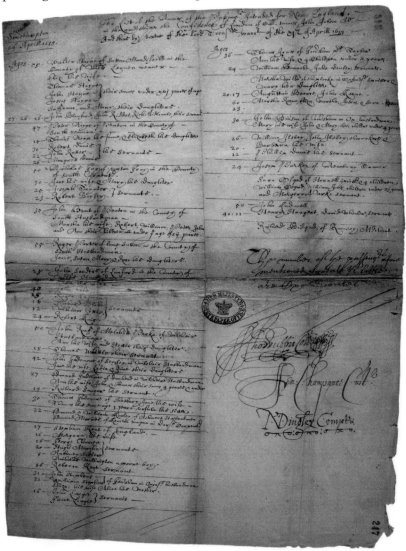

FIG. 6 *Passengers bound for New England in 1638.* CO 1/9

PROQuest (*www.proquest.com*) has produced a database of Colonial State Papers, which provides access to thousands of papers concerning the American, Canadian and West Indian colonies between the sixteenth and eighteenth centuries. All documents from CO 1, including maps, have been reproduced as full-colour, high-quality images digitized directly from the original documents.

1.3.3   *Treasury registers of passengers, 1773–6*
A useful, though short-lived, Treasury register (T 47/9–12) of emigrants leaving England, Wales and Scotland for the New World was kept by port customs officials between 1773 and 1776. For those visiting the National Archives, the information for England and Wales has been summarized in a card index, available in the Map and Large Document Room. This gives name, age, occupation, last place of residence, date of departure and destination, along with the reason for leaving the country. This series also includes names of passengers to Europe for this period.

1.4   Births, Marriages and Deaths

The National Archives not only houses records of departure but also of those passengers who were born, married or died on board vessels. These records were created following the Merchant Shipping Act 1854, which allowed for the compilation of births, deaths and marriages of passengers at sea from ships' official logs. The registers are quite full for the first two or three decades, as most emigrants travelled in the cheapest class of accommodation, known as steerage. The accommodation was frequently overcrowded and, with poor ventilation and long journeys, diseases such as cholera and typhus reached epidemic proportions. Many emigrants died as a result, particularly prior to the 1870s, by which time virtually all emigrants to North America and most to Australia travelled by steamship, which helped to cut journey times considerably. From about 1900 third class cabins replaced steerage accommodation and, although spartan, they were a considerable improvement on what had gone before.

Births, marriages and deaths at sea for the period 1854–83 and births and deaths only for the period 1883–90 can be found in the series BT 158 (Fig. 7). Masters were further required by the Registration of Births and Deaths Act 1874 to report births and deaths of both United Kingdom subjects and aliens to the Registrar General of Shipping. The information concerning United Kingdom subjects is in the series BT 160 Registers of Births of British Nationals at Sea and BT 159 Registers of Deaths of British Nationals at Sea. Records of later births and deaths at sea, for the period 1891–1964, are held in BT 334, with a marriage register for 1854–1972. Copies of some of these records are available to download (for a fee) at the commercial site *www.findmy-past.com*. Colonial Office returns of births and deaths at sea for the period 1847–54 and 1854–69 respectively can be found in the records of the Land and Emigration Commission in CO 386/170–2. Government Gazettes for Colonies can also include details of emigrants who died en route to their destinations. For example, CO 16/20 lists those who died aboard emigrant ships arriving in South Australia between 1849 and 1865 and was printed in the *South Australian Government Gazette* dated 25 January 1866.

1.5   Passenger Lists Held Elsewhere

1.5.1   *The United Kingdom*
The University of Liverpool has in its archives a small selection of outward passenger lists from the Cunard and White Star Shipping Lines. Very few passenger lists are included in their archive, but those that are cover the period 1840 to 1909 for voyages to Canada and the USA. For example, the University has three microfilms of passenger lists of the Cunard Line for the period 1840–53.

The Merseyside Maritime Museum Library and Archives, Albert Dock, Liverpool, holds diaries and fascinating letters of emigrants, family history notes and other official documents and correspondence including selected passenger lists and surgeons' reports.

No records of 'exit passes' of passengers or passenger application forms are known to survive in any UK archive.

1.5.2   *Europe*
The Hamburg State Archive in Germany holds lists of passengers sailing from the port of Hamburg to overseas destinations directly and indirectly, including the United Kingdom. These surviving lists cover the period from 1850 to 1934, with a break from 1914 to 1920 because of the First World War. The Latter-Day Saints (Mormon) Family History Library have copies of these lists on microfilm which can be ordered and seen in their Family History Centres. Their website (*www.familysearch.org*) indicates there are some 1,100 or so centres around the UK, with the main one at Hyde Park.

The direct and indirect lists for 1850–5 are arranged alphabetically by the first letter of the surname of the head of household. There are separate indexes for the direct and indirect lists from 1855 to 1910, and then a single index for both series from 1911. The indexes for 1855–1914 are arranged by the first letter of the surname of the head of the household, and then chronologically by the date the vessels sailed from Hamburg. The indexes for 1920–34 are in strict alphabetical order. A card index to the direct lists for the period 1850–71, and to the indirect lists for the years 1854–67, is held in the Hamburg State

Archive. The Latter-Day Saints Family History Library has a copy of this index on 46 microfilm reels. Most of the content can also be searched at *http://content.ancestry.com/iexec/?dbid=1068*.

1.5.3   *North America*

Most incoming passenger lists to the USA survive from 1820. Usually the following information is contained in these records: name of passenger, country or town of origin, date of arrival, intended destination, occupation, age and gender. Many of the passenger lists have been indexed, though there are important periods where no indexes exist, such as arrivals in New York from 1847 to 1897 and in Boston for 1820 to 1847 and again from 1892 to 1901. Where no indexes exist, the records are arranged chronologically and by port of arrival. For further information see the US National Archives website at *www. archives.gov/*. The website *www.ellisisland.org* allows you to search online over 22 million passengers and members of the ships' crews who came through Ellis Island and the port of New York between 1892 and 1924. Similarly, *www.castle-garden.org* offers free access to an extraordinary database of information on 10 million immigrants from 1830 to 1892, the year Ellis Island opened. Both can be searched by name and establish information relating to occupation, age, gender, literacy and last residence.

You should be aware that many emigrants migrated to the USA via Canada. For Canada, most passenger lists survive for the period 1865 to 1935 and they contain information such as name, age, country of origin, occupation and intended destination of passengers. From 1925 the lists contain additional information, including the immigrant's place of birth, the name and address of the relative, friend or employer to whom they were destined, and the name and address of the nearest relative in the country from which they came. For further information check the Library and Archives Canada website at *www.collections canada.gc.ca*. Some of these lists can be searched by passenger name using their online databases. See, for example, *http://www.collections canada.gc.ca/databases/immigration-1925/index-e.html*, which covers migration to Canada between 1925 and 1935. Many North American passenger lists are now available through commercial internet sites for a fee. For example, in September 2008, *www.ancestry.ca* put online all the Canadian passenger lists, 1865–1935.

Many of the earlier passenger lists to the New World have been transcribed and published either in print or online or on CD-ROM. Many were compiled from records available in the destination country, such as inwards ships' passenger lists and passenger cards, complementing and supplementing those records housed at the National Archives.

1.5.4   *Australasia*

Passenger lists for all ports in Australia survive from 1924, with some gaps. Earlier inwards passenger lists survive for the ports of Newcastle

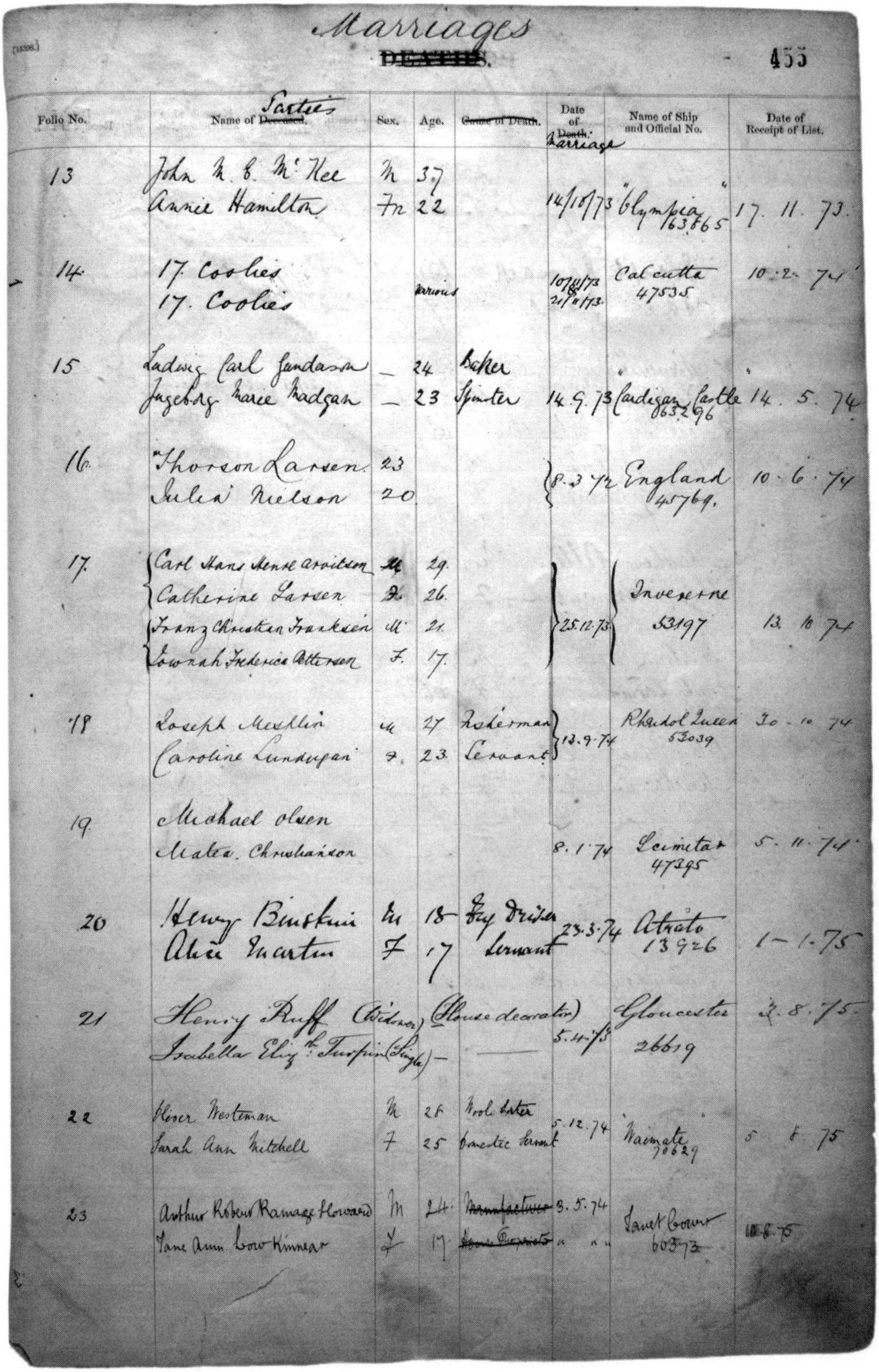

Folio No.	Name of Parties	Sex	Age	Cause of Death	Date of Marriage	Name of Ship and Official No.	Date of Receipt of List.
13	John M. C. McKee	M	37		14/10/73	Olympia 163865	17. 11. 73
	Annie Hamilton	Fn	22				
14	17. Coolies			various	10/8/73 21/10/73	Calcutta 47535	10. 2. 74
	17. Coolies						
15	Ludwig Carl Sandass	—	24	Baker	14.9.73	Cardigan Castle 63296	14. 5. 74
	Ingeborg Marie Madsen	—	23	Spinster			
16	Thorson Larsen		23		8.3.74	England 45769	10. 6. 74
	Julia Nielson		20				
17	Carl Hans Henre Arvilson	M	29		25.12.73	Inverene 53197	13. 10. 74
	Catherine Larsen	F	26				
	Franz Christen Franksen	M	21				
	Lovnah Frederica Otterson	F	17				
18	Joseph Mesllin	M	27	Fisherman	13.9.74	Rhidol Queen 53039	30. 10. 74
	Caroline Lundigan	F	23	Servant			
19	Michael Olsen				8.1.74	Scimitar 47295	5. 11. 74
	Mateo Christianson						
20	Henry Binskin	M	18	Fly Driver	23.3.74	Atrato 13926	1. 1. 75
	Alice Marten	F	17	Servant			
21	Henry Ruff (Widower)			(House decorator)	5.4.75	Gloucester 26619	3. 8. 75
	Isabella Eliz. Turpin (Single)		—	—			
22	Hover Westman	M	28	Wool Sorter	5.12.74	Waimate 70629	5. 6. 75
	Sarah Ann Mitchell	F	25	Domestic servant			
23	Arthur Robert Ramage Howard	M	24	Manufacturer	3.5.74	Janet Cover 60373	10.6.75
	Jane Ann Low Kinnear	F	17				

FIG. 7 Marriages recorded on British merchant vessels, 1873–5. BT 158/4

(for 1865–84), Darwin (1898–1934), Bowen (1897–1962), Brisbane (1852–1964), Cairns (from 1897), Hobart (from 1903), Rockhampton (from 1898), Townsville (from 1895) and Fremantle/Perth (from 1898). Further information is available at the National Archives of Australia website (*www.naa.gov.au*). Almost every Australian immigration record will be available online in the next few years thanks to the National Archives in Canberra. The Archives has committed to making records for the 7 million people who immigrated to Australia searchable on the internet, in a project likely to take several years.

A lot of work has already taken place. For example, the Record-Search part of its website which currently describes over 6 million records created by the Australian government – see *www.naa.gov.au/collection/recordsearch/index.aspx* – allows you to search for passengers arriving in Fremantle, Western Australia, by ship between January 1926 and 1947.

For New Zealand, most of the original passenger lists dating from the 1840s are held by Archives New Zealand in Thorndon, Wellington (*www.archives.govt.nz;* email: *reference@archives.gotv.net*). These lists were compiled by shipping companies and handed to a customs officer when the ship first arrived in New Zealand. The amount of information contained on these passenger lists varies, though most lists include the person's surname and initial, age, occupation and nationality. Lists prior to 1910 for the ports of Wellington, Auckland and Lyttelton and Bluff have been indexed by name, though those beyond 1910 have not and these lists are arranged chronologically and by port of arrival.

1.5.5 *Africa*
The National Archives of South Africa (*www.national.archives.gov.za;* email: *Archives@dac.gov.za*) provides a lot of information of use to family historians dating back to the seventeenth century, including records of settlers, but little is available online yet.

1.6 Passenger Lists Online

Regardless of where your ancestors came from, or went to, you may find an increasing number of websites of use and not mentioned above. Some charge for access, others do not. Some have transcripts of records and others have images of manifests to download. They include:

> *www.theshipslist.com* and *www.immigrantships.net* for ships' passenger lists.
> *www.cyndislist.com/ships.htm* for ships' passenger lists.
> *http://home.att.net/~arnielang/shipgide.html* for a research guide to United States immigration records and ships' passenger lists.
> *www.genealogy.com/genealogy/8_mgpal.html* for a guide to

locating ships' passenger lists.

http://home.att.net/~wee-monster/onlinelists.html for internet sources of transcribed passenger records and indexes.

http://home.att.net/~wee-monster/ei.html for emigration and immigration links.

http://home.att.net/~wee-monster/hamburg.html for Hamburg Passenger lists, 1850–1934.

www.blaxland.com/ozships for Australian arrivals and departures 1788–1967.

http://freepages.genealogy.rootsweb.com/~britishhomechildren for the essential site covering the British 'Home Children' who were sent to Canada between 1870 and 1940.

www.ellisisland.org to search online over 22 million passengers and members of the ships' crews who came through Ellis Island and the port of New York between 1892 and 1924.

www.ancestors.com and *www.ancestors.ca* to trace passengers to North America.

www.ancestors.com.au to trace emigrants to Australasia.

www.hamburg.de/LinkToYourRoots/english/welcome.htm for ancestors who might have emigrated from Europe to the New World via Hamburg.

olivetreegenealogy.com/index.shtml for passenger lists and much information about ships.

http://sa-passenger-list.za.net for passenger lists and settlers to South Africa, 1845–58.

www.castlegarden.org for a free database of US immigrants from 1830 to 1902.

http://aad.archives.gov.aad for records of passengers who arrived at the port of New York during the Irish Famine.

http://www.old-merseytimes.co.uk/PassengerLists.html for arrivals and departures from Liverpool, 1839–60.

1.7 Case Study

1.7.1 *Sarah Hurst*

Sometimes family historians can learn a gratifying amount about their ancestors thanks to the documents generated when things did not go quite to plan. Miss Sarah Stungo applied for her passport on 19 December 1916. Shortly afterwards she married Alfred Hurst, a naturalized British citizen who had been born in Romania. From his memorial papers (see 6.5) it is possible to learn that Alfred was a clerk at the firm of Louis Dreyfus & Co. It is also clear that he had been resident in the United Kingdom since he was 12 years old, attending a Council School in Old Castle Street, Aldgate, and that he applied to be naturalized as soon as he reached the age of majority nine years later.

Sarah and her new husband intended to travel to America to visit some of her relatives and booked places on the American Line steamer St Paul, which sailed from Liverpool on Saturday 30 December.

Unfortunately, as Sarah was now married a new passport was required, and a flurry of communication apparently began between her solicitors and the Passport Office as she tried to push her new application through over Christmas 1916. A note from her solicitors acknowledged that this must be 'an exceedingly busy' time, but suggested that they would see it as a 'personal favour' if her passport could be put in order in time. They also acknowledged that it might have been 'very much easier' if Sarah had allowed them to handle her first application as they would have certainly mentioned her pending nuptials.

Happily, Sarah received her passport on 29 December and the couple were able to make their journey as planned.

Relevant records include:

FO 737/24/11 Application Forms and Passport: Sarah Stungo Hurst 1916.

BT 27/876 Outward Passenger Lists (Liverpool), December, 1916 (including the list for *St Paul*) – available at *www.ancestorsonboard.com*.

HO 144/1094/196378 Nationality and Naturalization: Hershcovich, Avram (known as Alfred Hurst), from Roumania. Resident in London. Certificate 19544 issued 5 October 1910.

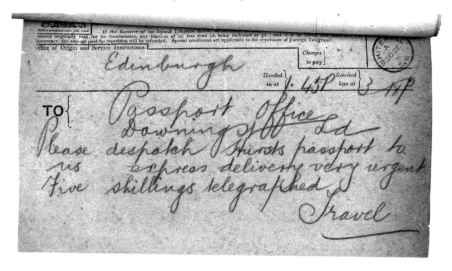

FIG. 8 *An urgent request for Sarah Hurst's replacement passport dated 28 December 1916.*
FO 737/24/11

2 EARLY TWENTIETH CENTURY MIGRATION

A wide range of people took the decision to leave their native countries in the first half of the twentieth century, a period scarred by two world wars. Prominent among them were refugees fleeing political or religious oppression. Others moved for economic reasons. Although many of those who came to this country in this period were absorbed into British society, wartime measures and the need for greater controls and restrictions have left a wide range of records for family historians to exploit.

2.1 General Sources

One major source for immigration records of the twentieth century is the Cabinet Office records, which include the conclusions and papers of the Cabinet and War Cabinets and their Committees. Here a two-year project (commenced in 2008) led by the National Archives and part-funded by the Joint Information Systems Committee (JISC) is particularly useful. This began in 2008 and is entitled British Governance in the 20th Century – Cabinet Papers, 1916–75. Its overall aim is to provide researchers, learners and teachers with comprehensive online access to the papers of Cabinet of the period.

These records, available through DocumentsOnline, comprise Cabinet Minutes and Conclusions and can be found in CAB 23 for 1916–39, CAB 65 for 1939–45 and CAB 129 after 1945. Cabinet Papers or Memoranda can be found in CAB 37 for 1880–1916, CAB 24 for 1916–39, CAB 66 for 1939–45 and CAB 129 after 1945. Paper copies of these records are in the Open Reading Room. The National Archives has also published several books about the papers of the Cabinet Office, which describe these records in great detail. These are also available for consultation in the Open Reading Room. Alternatively, you can refer to the CD-ROM *PROfiles* and the CD-ROM on the Macmillan years. Both are available on the public terminals using OPERA (Online publications and electronic resources).

Other central government records concerning 'aliens' and refugees may be found among Prime Minister's Office (PREM) papers. Correspondence and papers from 1916 to 1940 are in PREM 1. Files from 1940 to 1945 are in PREM 3. General correspondence and papers from 1945 to 1951 are in PREM 8 and from 1951 to 1964 in PREM 11. The series continues after 1964 in PREM 13.

General policy matters and files concerning aliens, refugees, internees and deportees in the twentieth century can be found among Home Office series, specifically HO 45 (Registered Papers) and HO 144 (Registered Papers: supplementary) for the period before 1920, and HO 213 (Aliens Department: general and aliens' naturalization and nationality files) for the period thereafter. All three series contain general policy files and deal with the definition of British and foreign nationality, immigration, refugees, internees and prisoners of war, deportation and related subjects.

Other related series containing general policy files for these subjects include HO 352, HO 355 and HO 367. In 1962 the Aliens Department was merged with the Naturalization and Nationality Division and renamed the Immigration and Nationality Department, and files for this period can be found in HO 394.

The indexes to the general correspondence of the Foreign Office (FO) also contain information relating to the arrival of aliens and refugees in the twentieth century. The period 1906 to 1919 is covered by a card index in the Open Reading Room. From 1920 to 1951 the index is in the form of printed volumes, also held here, and for the years 1952, 1953 and 1959 there are similar non-published departmental indexes that can be found in the Open Reading Room. These indexes mainly refer to papers in FO 371 Political Departments, but some refer to other departments, such as FO 369 Consular Department, FO 370 Library and Research Departments, FO 372 Treaty Department and FO 395 News Department. For the years 1954 to 1958 and 1960 to 1966 there are no detailed indexes in these series and it is necessary to consult the relevant series lists to access the records. From 1967 to October 1968, when the Foreign and Commonwealth Office was formed, the political departments of the Foreign Office operated a common registry with the Commonwealth Office and the Diplomatic Service Administration Office, and records from this period can be found in various FCO series by department.

Records of the Metropolitan Police Office in MEPO 2 and MEPO 3 include policy files relating to the administration of the Aliens Act 1914. Policy and welfare matters dealt with by the Ministry of Labour can be found in LAB 8 and LAB 26. See 2.3.2 and 2.3.3 for more details. The National Archives also holds records of the British Council, relating to the promotion of Great Britain and the English language abroad and the development of closer cultural and commercial links with other countries. BW 108 contains correspondence and papers relating to London centres or 'hearths', set up to make visitors feel welcome. Only records relating to the London centres are known to have survived. Correspondence includes records relating to Polish, Yugoslavian and Dutch hearths. Files cover the period 1942–6, after which British Council responsibility came to an end.

2.2 The Impact of Legislation

A Royal Commission on Alien Immigration was set up in 1903 to look into the subject of immigration. This found that only deck passengers were subject to any kind of examination by local customs officers, and once landed, aliens were subject to no further restrictions and no registration was called for.

The 1905 Aliens Act (5 Edw. VII c. 13) provided for a new system of regulation and control, but there is still a general paucity of records. The outbreak of the First World War, however, prompted tighter legislation. The Aliens Registration Act 1914 made registration with the police mandatory for all aliens over the age of 16, providing the government with accurate information concerning the profession, age, race and location of aliens who were resident in the country. Under the British Nationality and Status Act (4 and 5 Geo. V c. 17) the statutory qualification of applicants was extended to record that applicants must be of good character and must have an adequate knowledge of English.

With the enactment of the Aliens Order of 1920, the Immigration Branch of the Home Office was set up and the country was divided into districts: Newcastle, Hull, Harwich, London, Dover, Southampton and Bristol, each supervised by an Inspector. Scotland and Northern Ireland were looked after by a Chief Immigration Officer, stationed at Glasgow.

The role of the inspectors was to enforce immigration legislation and control at ports until humanitarian considerations in the 1930s raised by the influx of refugees from Nazi Germany began to have an impact. These led to a relaxation of the Aliens Order until the entire nature of the Immigration Service's work altered with the outbreak of the Second World War.

2.3 Records Relating to Aliens

The early twentieth century saw the growth of some established communities through new arrivals. Jewish refugees, for example, travelled to Britain from Germany, Poland and Russia between 1887 and 1905. Files relating to these can be found in HO 45 and MEPO 2, while records of the Jews' Temporary Shelter, set up by the Jewish community to help the newcomers, are held in the London Metropolitan Archives.

Other less established communities continued to grow. In some cases

FIG. 9 *A family of Jewish immigrants at their Seder table in the early twentieth century.*

their small size belied the extent to which they would blossom in the second half of the century.

Records to some distinct groups can be hard to find, but are often there if you know where to look for them. The Asia, Pacific and Africa collection of the British Library, for example, contains scattered reference to the provision that was made in the early twentieth centuries for destitute Indians in the UK in (LP J/6 and J/7). These people, who included seamen and discharged servants, appear to have become stranded in Britain and so were, effectively, immigrants. The indexes to these records include names of individuals.

Two world wars prompted a focus on the foreign population and generated records on a scale that had not been seen before. Those that survive and are accessible are an enormous boon to researchers. Often details of ordinary people can be found to a level that would previously only have been left by those rich enough to afford to become naturalized or obtain letter patent.

2.3.1 Home Office records

A personal file was opened on any alien who had contact with the Home Office and then maintained from the initial visa or employment application through to an application for naturalization or death. The majority of aliens files have been destroyed under a Home Office disposal schedule, but happily a number survive and these can be found in HO 382 and HO 405.

The series HO 382 consists of personal files for individuals entering or trying to enter the United Kingdom after 1935. These files have been selected either to illustrate the operation of the Home Office procedures or because they relate to famous individuals. There are, for example, files relating to William Joyce – Lord Haw Haw – and his wife Margaret, the US singer Paul Robeson and Soviet politician Leon Trotsky. This is an accruing series and may have more cases added to it, either because the individual is famous and the file may add to what is known of them (i.e. sources for biographers) or as a specimen file to illustrate how the Home Office handled various aspects of immigration control and how immigration policy was applied in actual cases.

The selection of pre-Second World War files has been generous, to show how the Home Office handled those refugees from Nazism who did not settle here. The series is being expanded to include a relatively large number of Cold War files – mainly of socialist refugees who lived here during the Second World War and returned home, only to return as refugees from Stalinism. Many of them failed to obtain naturalization.

The series HO 405 is very different in its scope. This contains files opened on individual foreign citizens (mostly European) who arrived in the UK and who applied for naturalization. These cover the period 1934–48 and include applications for naturalization with police reports. Some also include initial applications for visa or employment permit, changes of name or business name and Second World War internment papers. Files were opened when the individual first applied to enter the UK and continued until naturalization or death.

HO 405 is being transferred gradually according to initial surname of alien. Those covering surnames A–N have been transferred and are searchable by name of alien and date of birth on the Catalogue. It is important to note that this series is closed for 100 years. However, you can request a review of closed records by following the prompts at piece level description in the Catalogue. The Home Office will also continue to respond to enquiries relating to records not yet transferred. It will be many years before all the files are at the National Archives and many more before they are fully available.

Files in HO 405 relating to married couples are listed under the name of the husband, and the wife's file is attached to the husband's. Spelling of names sometimes varies throughout the files. The name listed is that used on the naturalization certificate (where issued) and other names are noted as 'aka' or 'formerly'. All possible variants of a name should be used when a search is being conducted.

The series HO 5 could prove a useful source if you are researching ancestors or relatives in the earlier part of the century. This includes out-letters and entry books of the Home Office and the Aliens Office relating to topics from applications for naturalization to the issuing of alien certificates. The series covers the period 1794 to 1921. Original documents can be viewed at the National Archives or searched by name and downloaded at *www.ancestry.co.uk*.

2.3.2 Police records

Compulsory registration with the police was first introduced under the provisions of the Aliens Registration Act 1914. As a result of this legislation, aliens were obliged to provide detailed particulars, including name, address, marital status, employment or occupation, employer's name and address and a photograph, and had to pay a registration fee. A registered person was also required to register changes of address, marital status, nationality and occupation. In return the alien received a police certificate of registration.

Registers of aliens, where they survive, can be found locally at either county record offices or police archives. No central register of aliens survives, though HO 45/10831/326287 and HO 45/11522/287235 consist of policy and administrative papers in respect of the register. MEPO 35 Metropolitan Police: Aliens Registration Office: Sample Record Cards contains the surviving aliens' registration cards for the London area. The 104 files in this series account for some 1,000 cases out of the tens of thousands of aliens resident in London since 1914. Although the cards represent a small sample they do include some notable cases, such as Joe Coral the bookmaker (MEPO 35/16/1). The surviving records show a heavy concentration of cases around the late 1930s, as Germans and east Europeans fled the Nazi persecutions.

The cards are rich in information, giving full name, date of birth, date of arrival into the UK, employment history, address, marital status, details of any children and (if applicable) the date of naturalization with Home Office reference. The cards usually include at least one photograph, and for some cases there are continuation cards. Records for individuals known to have died or to have been born more than 100 years ago can be searched and viewed through DocumentsOnline.

Although MEPO 2 and MEPO 3 largely consist of policy files, some records do include details of resident aliens. For example, MEPO 3/2435 contains returns and reports on aliens holding liquor licences or employed in licensed houses in London Metropolitan Police districts during the First World War. Also, MEPO 2/1796 includes a list of German nationals resident in London who applied for the return of their property sequestrated by the government during the First World War.

2.3.3 Ministry of Labour records

LAB 8 and LAB 26 consist of files relating to general policy and welfare matters dealt with by the Ministry of Labour. They include a variety of subjects, such as accommodation of workers, particularly for immigrant post-Second World War refugees and other foreign nationals; the recruitment of foreigners to work in Britain; hostels; housing estates for Polish workers; clubs and other recreational centres. Specimen applications from aliens for work permits can be found in LAB 900/1 and LAB 48. The latter consists of applications from aliens between 1968 and 1975. These records are all open and can be searched by name on the Catalogue.

2.4 Internees in the First World War

Very few records of individual internees survive for the First World War. Lists of names of internees were routinely forwarded to the Prisoners of War Information Bureau in London, which in turn informed the International Red Cross Headquarters in Geneva. The lists compiled by the Bureau were largely destroyed by bombing in 1940. However, two specimen lists of German subjects interned as POWs in the brief period 1915–16 can be found in WO 900/45 and 46. The list is divided into army, naval and civilian prisoners, and gives the regiment, ship or home address of each prisoner.

A classified list of aliens assessed for internment but not interned can be found in HO 144/11720/364868. Nominal rolls of male enemy aliens of the age of 45 and upwards, submitted to the Secretary of State by commandants of internment camps, are included among a census of aliens resident in the United Kingdom between 1915 and 1924 in HO 45/11522/287235. Lists of alien enemies detained in Lunatic Asylums within the Metropolitan Police District can also be found in this document, though there is no name index. Appeals against internment can be found among the older papers attached to some of the files in HO 405 (see 2.3.1).

FIG. 11 *Categories applied to German males assessed for internment in 1914.* HO 144/11720/364868

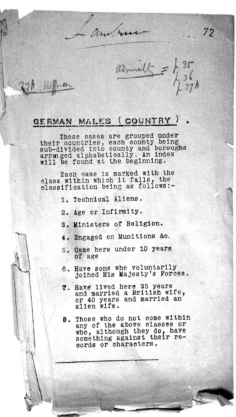

References to individual internees can also be found in the card index to the Foreign Office general correspondence in the Open Reading Room.

Information of a more general nature relating to internees and internment camps can be found in HO 45 and HO 144. For example, HO 45/10946/266042 and HO 45/10947/266042 both relate to administration of internment camps on the Isle of Man, one of the key locations for such camps within Britain.

Other material on internees can be found in correspondence of the Metropolitan Police in MEPO 2. This includes MEPO 2/1633, which consists of the administration of Islington Internment Camp during the First World War.

2.5 Refugees from Belgium, 1914–19

Shortly after the outbreak of the First World War, Britain was called upon to make provision for very large numbers of homeless refugees from Belgium. The War Refugees Committee established a scheme to remove women and children deemed particularly under threat and place them under conditions of safekeeping in Britain. A special department was formed at the Local Government Board to deal with all questions relating to war refugees, including registration, hospitality, employment, hostels and refuges, transport and repatriation.

The chief refugee camps were in London at Alexandra Palace, Earl's Court, the Edmonton Refuge and Millfield House, and these various London refuges provided accommodation for a total of 10,000 refugees. The camps were administered internally by the refugees themselves, and their facilities included resident medical officers, schools, chapels, playrooms and cinemas.

In October 1914 it was decided that a central register of Belgian refugees should be kept. The resulting register recorded a total of roughly 260,000 names by 1919. Valuable information about employment and unemployment among the refugees was also obtained, as well as information about Belgians of military age, which was required by the Belgian military authorities.

The vast majority of refugees were housed across England and Wales, where some 2,500 Local Representative Committees were set up. Records relating to the work of these committees will be found in local record offices. Scotland received upwards of 18,000 refugees of whom some 1,500 were sent to Glasgow direct from the port of arrival without passing through the London refuges.

The refugees included a considerable number of Jews, especially from Antwerp, who were cared for by the Jewish Society, later the Jewish War Refugees Committee. For further information see the Hartley Library, University of Southampton (*www.soton.ac.uk/library*).

Background papers relating to the work undertaken by the British government in the reception and care of Belgian refugees can be found in HO 45.

The series MH 8 War Refugees Committee contains a selection of minutes, hostel lists, statistics, correspondence and other documents including history cards. The last of these could offer a considerable amount of information. Each relates to a whole family filed by the name of its head, unless the refugee was single with no known relatives, giving names, ages, relationships, spouse's maiden name, allowances and the address for payment.

Specimen registration forms for Belgian refugees can be found in RG 20/86 and MH 8/6–7.

2.6   Jewish Refugees from Europe

In the 1930s as Jewish refugees began to arrive in the UK from Germany and Austria, it was initially argued that the current high levels of unemployment demanded a cautious approach. Entry was therefore granted predominantly to those refugees who had the prospect of permanent immigration elsewhere. Camps were set up, such as the Kitchener Camp for Poor Persons in Kent, to house Jewish refugees temporarily pending re-emigration to other countries. Here, over 3,000 Jewish refugees were housed in 1939.

A selection of files on refugees who settled in the UK for the period 1934–48 are in the process of being transferred from the Home Office in series HO 405 and these include records relating to Jewish refugees – see 2.3.1 for more details. Similarly, MEPO 35 Metropolitan Police: Aliens Registration Office: Sample Record Cards includes a heavy concentration of cases around the late 1930s, as Germans and east Europeans fled the Nazi persecutions (see 2.3.2).

After the *Anschluss* of March 1938, the British government, fearing an influx of refugees that might overwhelm voluntary organizations and create public resentment, put a visa system in place for German and Austrian refugees. Reluctant to admit a large number of refugees to Britain itself, the government began to look for suitable centres for settlement within the Empire. The Evian Conference in July 1938 sought a coordinated international solution to the question, but nothing of substance emerged. Many had been admitted to Palestine, which had been designated a British mandated territory in 1920, but here the 1937 Peel Commission recommended that no more than 12,000 Jewish immigrants each year should be admitted for fear of Arab reactions to the new arrivals.

Jewish records are also held elsewhere. Most of the refugees settled in or around London, and the records of the Jewish Temporary Shelter are available at the London Metropolitan Archives. A highly significant holding of records are still kept by the Jewish Refugees Committee at Drayton House, Gordon Street, London but access is usually restricted to the individuals themselves or next of kin.

The Moving Here website *www.movinghere.org.uk* includes in-depth resources, including exhibitions, galleries and online records both within and outside the National Archives, celebrating Jewish migration to England. The online records include many alien internee tribunal cards for mainly Jewish refugees in HO 396.

2.7   The Czechoslovak Refugee Trust

It is worth checking the files of the Czechoslovak Refugee Trust in HO 294 if the person you are researching travelled from Czechoslovakia, even if they were not a Czechoslovak citizen. The Trust was created on 21 July 1939 and wound up in 1975. Its original purpose was the assistance of those who sought refuge from Nazi persecution following the ceding to Germany of parts of the territory of Czechoslovakia under the Munich Agreement of 30 September 1938 and the subsequent dismemberment of that country by the Germans in March 1939. These included not only Czechoslovak citizens but also several hundred Germans and Austrians who had gained asylum in Czechoslovakia after escaping Nazi persecution in their own countries between 1933 and 1938.

Before the Trust was created, several appeals had been launched in Britain for subscriptions for the relief of the refugees, among them those by the Lord Mayor of London, and the *News Chronicle* and *Manchester Guardian* newspapers. Some of the money raised was set aside for the use of the London-based British Committee for Refugees from Czechoslovakia, a voluntary organization set up in October 1938 to provide temporary hospitality in Britain for especially endangered refugees. British government policy was that the refugees could be accepted in Britain only as transmigrants. Between October 1938 and March 1939 the British Committee brought 3,500 refugees from Czechoslovakia to Britain, which absorbed all the financial resources available to the Committee.

In practice the Trust took over where the British Committee left off for want of funds, and when the Czechoslovak government Refugee Department was forced to discontinue operations. The assistance to be afforded to refugees took two forms:

Emigration to some overseas country of settlement
Maintenance and training in Britain pending re-emigration.

Permanent settlement of refugees was possible on only a very restricted scale during the war, but by the end of 1947 the resettlement of refugees from Nazism had been substantially achieved across Europe.

In February 1948, however, a new category of refugees was created following the coup d'état by which a Communist regime was established in Czechoslovakia, and the British government enlarged the categories of Trust beneficiaries to include refugees from that regime.

The Trust was wound up in 1975 when the Charity Commissioners agreed that the administration of the Fund should pass to the Trustees of the British Council for Aid to Refugees.

HO 294/1–234 relates to policy and administration of the fund. Specimen personal files of refugee families in the various categories are in HO 294/235–486. Case papers of other refugee families, extracted from files that have not been preserved, are in HO 294/487–611: in many instances these provide a detailed case history. A numerical index to cases (HO 294/612–13) is open to readers, but the family files and case papers are closed for 50, or in some instances 75, years, though requests for reviews are possible under the Freedom of Information Act 2000.

Related files may be found in FO 371, T 210 (Czechoslovak Financial Claims Office: Files), HO 213 and HO 352/139–40. Also, personal files for some have been selected for HO 405 (see 2.3.1 for further details).

2.8 Internment in the Second World War

With the declaration of war on 3 September 1939, some 70,000 UK resident Germans and Austrians found themselves classed as enemy aliens. By the end of the month, the Aliens Department of the Home Office had set up internment tribunals throughout the country, each headed by government officials and local representatives, to examine every UK registered enemy alien over the age of 16. The object was to divide the aliens into three categories: Category A, to be interned; Category B, to be exempt from internment but subject to the restrictions decreed by the Special Order; and Category C, to be exempt from both internment and restrictions.

Some 120 tribunals were established, assigned to different regions of the UK. Many were established within London, where large numbers of Germans and Austrians resided. There were 11 set up in northwest London alone. The police were responsible for providing the details of enemy aliens to the tribunals, as they kept registers of aliens, a requirement since the 1914 Aliens Registration Act (4 and 5 Geo. V c. 12).

By February 1940 nearly all the tribunals had completed their work assessing some 73,000 cases. The vast majority (some 66,000) of enemy aliens were classed as Category C. This figure included most, but by no means all, of the 55,000 Jewish refugees who had come to the UK to escape Nazi persecution in the early and mid-1930s. Of the remainder, some 6,700 were classified as Category B and 569 as A. Those classified in Category A were interned in camps being set up across the UK, the largest settlements of which were on the Isle of Man, though others were also set up in and around Glasgow, Liverpool, Manchester, Bury, Huyton, Sutton Coldfield, London, Kempton Park, Ling-field, Seaton and Paignton.

However, by May 1940, with the risk of German invasion high, regardless of their Category classification, a further 8,000 Germans and Austrians resident in the southern strip of England found themselves interned. Resident Italians were also considered for internment following Italy's declaration of war on Britain on 10 June 1940. Some 4,000 resident Italians who were known to be members of the Italian Fascist Party, and others aged between 16 and 70 who had lived in the UK for less than 20 years, were ordered to be interned.

The increase in numbers of those interned led to a serious space problem within the UK and, following offers from the Canadian and Australian governments, more than 7,500 internees were shipped overseas on 24 June and 1, 2, 4 and 10 July 1940 on the vessels *Ettrick*, *Sobieski*, *Duchess of York*, *Dunera* and *Arandora Star*. Tragically, on 2 July 1940, the *Arandora Star* was torpedoed and sunk in the Atlantic en route to Canada. On board were 712 Italians, 438 Germans (including both Nazi sympathizers and Jewish refugees), and 374 British seamen and soldiers. Over half lost their lives. It was this event that swayed public sympathy towards the enemy aliens. There are further papers relating to those interned overseas, including an embarkation list for the *Arandora Star* (HO 215/438), the *Dunera* (HO 215/1), the *Ettrick* (HO 215/267) and the *Sobieski* (HO 215/266).

The release of 1,687 Category C and B enemy aliens was authorized in August 1940, and by October of that year about 5,000 Germans, Austrians and Italians had been released following the publication of a White Paper by the Under-Secretary of the Home Office, Osbert Peake. Titled *Civilian Internees of Enemy Nationality*, the Paper identified categories of persons who could be eligible for release. By December, the number had risen to 8,000, though this left some 19,000 still interned in camps in Britain, Canada and Australia. Of those released, some 1,273 were men who applied to join the Pioneer Corps. They would be joined by internees in Canada and Australia, but here the process of release would take longer. By March 1941, 12,500 internees had been released, rising to over 17,500 in August, and by 1942 fewer than 5,000 remained interned, mainly on the Isle of Man.

2.8.1 *Personal records*

The series HO 396 consists of index cards for the Internees Tribunals set up in September 1939. The records run through to 1947, are usually grouped by category depending on whether people were exempted from internment or interned, and by nationality. Within categories they are arranged in alphabetical order by surname.

The papers provide personal information on the front, such as full name, date and place of birth, nationality, address, occupation, name and address of employer and decision of the tribunal. The reason for the tribunal's decision is usually noted on the reverse of the card.

The cards have all been microfilmed and those cases deemed exempt from internment (Category B and C) have been made available free as digital images on the Moving Here website *www.movinghere.org.uk*. The records can be searched by name.

The remainder of the series relates to people who were at some stage interned and these are available on microfilm at the National Archives. The reverse of cards for those interned provides information about the time of internment. This information is closed for 85 years, though under the Freedom of Information Act 2000, it is possible to request a review of the information.

Information on those internees shipped out to Canada and to Australia can be found in the series HO 396/107–14 and HO 396/139–45 respectively. These give name, date of birth and the name of the internee ships, with dates of embarkation. If you are researching someone who was, for example, interned in the UK, then shipped to Canada and finally released from internment before returning to this country, you should remember that they may have cards in several places.

The series HO 405 relates to individual foreign citizens (mostly European) who arrived in the UK between 1934 and 1948 and who applied for naturalization. All files include applications for naturalization with police reports. Some also include initial applications for visa or employment permit, change of name or business name and Second World War internment papers, as many internees remained in the UK after the war and applied for British nationality in the post-war years. For further information see 2.3.1.

Similarly, further records of internees can be found in the series MEPO 35. This series contains the surviving aliens' registration cards for the London area. These represent some 1,000 cases out of the tens of thousands of aliens resident in London since 1914 and appear to show a heavy concentration of cases around the late 1930s, as Germans and east Europeans fled the Nazi persecutions. The information provided on the cards includes full name, date of birth, date of arrival into the UK, employment history, address, marital status, details of any children, and date of naturalization, with Home Office reference if applicable. They also include reference to internee tribunals and internment. The cards usually include at least one photograph and for some cases there are continuation cards. See 2.3.2 for more information.

Details of internees shipped overseas can be found in BT 27 for outward journeys and BT 26 for return journeys. These series of passenger lists are available to search and download on the sites *www.ancestors onboard.com* and *www.ancestry.co.uk* respectively. The information given in these lists includes the age, occupation and address in the United Kingdom and the date of entering or departing the United King-

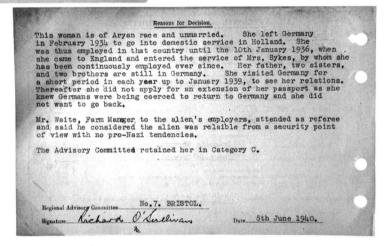

REGIONAL ADVISORY COMMITTEE

APPEAL DECISION   NON-REFUGEE—FEMALE

(1) Surname (block capitals) ___ WEILER,

   Forenames ___ Johanna Emilie

   Alias ___

(2) Date and place of birth ___ 19th October 1909 : Bochum, Germany. B.W.

(3) Nationality ___ German.

(4) Police Regn. Cert. No. ___ 577698.   Home Office reference, if known ___ AGH GP.

(5) Address ___ "The Chantry", Chute, Nr. Andover, Wiltshire.

2|09

(6) Normal occupation ___ Domestic Servant.   OCC. GP.

(7) Present Occupation ___ Domestic Servant.

(8) Decision of Tribunal   ~~Left subject to 6A & 9A~~ } Strike out which do not apply.   EX. 6A.
   ~~Left subject to 9A~~   and 9A
   Exempt from 6A & 9A

(9) Decision of Advisory Committee   Exempted from 6A & 9A } Strike out which does not apply.
   ~~Left subject to 6A & 9A~~

*[8257] 51355/590 53m (8 sorts) 3/40 4070 G & S 704   [OVER

FIG. 12 *The front and reverse of an Internment Tribunal card from June 1940.* HO 396/98

Reasons for Decision.

This woman is of Aryan race and unmarried. She left Germany in February 1934 to go into domestic service in Holland. She was thus employed in that country until the 10th January 1936, when she came to England and entered the service of Mrs, Sykes, by whom she has been continuously employed ever since. Her father, two sisters, and two brothers are still in Germany. She visited Germany for a short period in each year up to January 1939, to see her relations. Thereafter she did not apply for an extension of her passport as she knew Germans were being coerced to return to Germany and she did not want to go back.

Mr. Waite, Farm Manager to the alien's employers, attended as referee and said he considered the alien was reliable from a security point of view with no pro-Nazi tendencies.

The Advisory Committee retained her in Category C.

Regional Advisory Committee   No.7. BRISTOL.

Signature   *Richard O'Sullivan*   Date   8th June 1940.

dom by sea from or to ports outside Europe and the Mediterranean. See 1.2.4 and 1.1.3 for more information about these records.

2.8.2   Life in the camps

The Home Office had overall responsibility for the welfare of internees and, from August 1940 onwards, for the internal management and the administration of the camps in which they were kept (the War Office retained responsibility for security and the provision of guards). The series HO 215 relates to the treatment of internees during their period of internment, the health and educational facilities which they were afforded, their movement within the United Kingdom and abroad, their release and in some cases repatriation, and the conditions in and administration of the camps. The series contains several examples of reports by the International Red Cross and by Swiss legations on the conditions in internment camps in the United Kingdom and the dominions and also on prisoner-of-war and internment camps in enemy and enemy-occupied countries. The latter were sent to the Foreign Office and forwarded to the Home Office in order that a check could be maintained on the conditions under which British nationals were being held abroad.

When camps were established they were often separated into camps for men and camps for women and children. HO 215/365–6 details the policy of children joining interned mothers on the Isle of Man. HO 215 also includes nominal rolls of internees in the Hutchinson, Metropole, Mooragh, Onchan and Port Erin camps on the Isle of Man. It also includes lists of those repatriated to Germany in 1945. Other documents, such as HO 215/169, which details the problems caused by placing German and Italian Jews with gentile prisoners in Perveril Camp on the Isle of Man, may also be of interest.

HO 213 is a broader series containing policy files relating to the definition of British and foreign nationality, naturalizations, immigration, refugees, internees and prisoners of war, the employment of foreign labour, deportation, the status of citizens of the Irish Republic, and related subjects. There are also papers relating to departmental committees, statistics, conferences, conventions and treaties on these subjects. It contains fascinating files on internment, including the document HO 213/1053, which includes photographs of internees and a report of an inspection of camps on the Isle of Man, focusing on women, children and married couples interned there (Fig. 13). Commandants of camps would set up industries (such as glove-making or farm work) and internees were allowed to create their own entertainment, staging plays, concerts and showing films. Many of those interned were artistic, including actors, writers, artists and musicians.

Local county archives also hold records relating to internment camps and internees. Check the A2A website *www.nationalarchives. gov.uk/a2a*. The A2A database contains catalogues describing archives held throughout England and dating from the 900s to the present day. The Manx National Heritage Library, Manx Museum, Douglas, Isle of Man, IM1 3LY (tel: 01624 648000, *www.gov.im/mnh*) holds its own records relating to internment on the Isle of Man in both the First and Second World Wars. Finally, the Anglo-German Family History Society (*www.agfhs.org*) is a useful contact for all those who are interested in researching the genealogy or family history of people from the German-speaking parts of Europe who have emigrated over the centuries and settled in the UK. The Society has published material relating to internees. Similarly, the Anglo-Italian Family History Society (*www.anglo-italian.org.uk*) is useful in finding out more about Italian internees.

2.9   Prisoners of War

Very few records of individual enemy prisoners of war survive for the First World War. Far more survives for the Second World War, and what survives is also likely to be of far more interest to family historians.

Normally, POWs are returned to their homeland on the conclusion of hostilities. In May 1945, however, it was found that many of the 'German' POWs in the UK were actually people of various central European origins who had been pressed into service with the Nazi war machine. Not all of these wanted to be repatriated from the UK. Of the POWs captured in German uniform who were given the option to remain in the UK, almost 20,000 men did. Those who availed themselves of this concession were released from POW status and placed on conditions that tied them to agricultural duties.

Correspondence with the United States authorities on policy concerning POWs in general can be found among the papers of the British Joint Staff Mission in Washington (CAB 122). The Operational Papers of the Prime Minister's Office (the Churchill Papers), PREM 3/363–4, contain material relating to both enemy and allied POWs. Correspondence between the British government, the Red Cross and the Protecting Powers, including inspection reports on UK POW camps, is among the records of the Consular (War) Department of the Foreign Office, in FO 916. The few surviving records of the Prisoners of War Information Bureau itself are in WO 307. The files in CO 968/33–6 contain correspondence of the Colonial Office Defence section relating to internment policy in the British colonies and includes lists of enemy POWs in various colonial territories.

2.9.1   *Records relating to individuals*
Lists of names of enemy prisoners were routinely forwarded to the Prisoners of War Information Bureau in London, which in turn informed the International Red Cross (ICRC) Headquarters in Geneva. The lists compiled for the Bureau were largely destroyed by bombing in 1940. However, two surviving lists of German subjects interned as POWs in 1915–16 can be found in WO 900/45 and 46. These are divided into army, naval and civilian prisoners, and give the regiment, ship or home address of each prisoner.

Online application can also be made on the ICRC Archives website *www.icrc.org/eng/contact-archives*. An hourly search fee is charged unless the request is made by the individual concerned or their family. You should allow up to four months for a reply.

Correspondence about enemy merchant seamen taken prisoner is in MT 9. Files concerning the employment of enemy POWs in Britain are among the records of the Ministry of National Service (Labour Supply Department), and can be found in NATS 1/567–71.

A substantial amount of material relating to POWs (British, allied and enemy) is contained in the General Political Correspondence of the Foreign Office in FO 371. References to individuals can be found in the Foreign Office General Correspondence (1906–19) card index, which is located in the Open Reading Room. In addition, FO 566/1837–74 contains 'Prisoners and Aliens Registers, 1915–1919', arranged by country. A large proportion of this correspondence has not survived.

Registered Papers concerning prisoners both during and after the Second World War are in WO 32. The Medical Historian's Papers in WO 222 include reports on the health of POWs and on the work of POW hospitals. The War Diary of MI19, the division of Military Intelligence responsible for the interrogation of enemy POWs, is in WO 165/41. Records of the Combined Services Detailed Interrogation Centre (CSDIC) and of the Prisoners of War Interrogation Section can be found in WO 208. Many of these files are closed for 75 years, although the CSDIC reports in WO 208/4117–212 are now open. A few interrogation reports made on German POWs in 1944 exist in the files of the Control Commission for Germany: Internal Affairs and Communications Division, in FO 1050/169. Interrogation reports on enemy airmen among the records of the Air Ministry's Directorate of Intelligence (AIR 40) are closed for 75 years. Some debriefings of enemy POWs can be found in the files concerning the Prisoners of War Campaign conducted by the Political Warfare Executive of the Foreign Office, in FO 898/320–30.

Nominal lists of enemy POWs who were temporarily interned in the Tower of London can be found in WO 94/105.

2.9.2   *Information on camps*

War diaries of units of the British Army contain material on POW camps, labour companies, etc. in various theatres of war. These can in most cases be identified from the indexes to the appropriate series lists. The war diaries of the Directorate of Prisoners of War are in WO 165/59–71, and minutes and reports of the Imperial Prisoners of War Committee meetings can also be found there. Some selected war diaries of hospitals, depots and camps are in WO 177/1833–55, and selected unit day-to-day operational diaries of POW camps can be found in WO 166; there is a general index at the beginning of this series.

Numerous files on individual POW camps in the United Kingdom are among the records of the Prisoners of War Section of the London-based Control Office for Germany and Austria (FO 939). Lists of POW and internment camps are among the Military Headquarters Papers: Home Forces, in WO 199/404–9.

2.10   Operation 'Post Reports'

Policy records relating to Operation 'Post Reports' (OPR) can be found in HO 355 Home Office: Immigration Branch: AIB and IBR (Symbol Series) Files. These records include the interviewing of Hungarian and Italian refugees. Most of these files are retained by the Home Office Department under Section 3.4 of the Public Records Act.

Several thousand of the reports themselves are, however, in the early stages of being transferred. They date from the 1940s and 1950s and

FIG. 13 *Women interned on the Isle of Man during the Second World War.* HO 213/1053

cover those foreign nationals living in the UK at the outbreak of the Second World War who were required to report to the Aliens Office for an assessment of their security risk. Each OPR consists of one sheet of paper containing some of the following details: Home Office reference number (which will link to surviving aliens' files in HO 405 or HO 382), passport number, police registration number, landing conditions and address. This information is then followed by an assessment of the individual's security risk, carried out by the Special Branch. Some of the OPRs list relatives' names, occupation and town of residence.

Because of the sensitive nature of many of the reports, they are likely to be transferred as closed during the lifetime of the individuals concerned or until they can be assumed to be deceased (i.e. their 100th birthday). Under the Freedom of Information Act 2000, you will be able to request a review by using the Request Review link at piece level description in the Catalogue.

2.11 Deportees

The power to expel aliens who had become paupers or criminals was first given under the Aliens Act 1905, and continued under subsequent amendments to the Act and an Order in Council made in 1920.

Courts could recommend the deportation of an alien found guilty of certain specified crimes or of an offence for which a fine could not be substituted for imprisonment. Deportation could be recommended in addition to or in lieu of sentence. The Home Secretary was not bound to act on the recommendation of the court and might decide not to make an expulsion order – for example, in cases where a person had been resident for a long time or might suffer political persecution on return to the native country. In addition, he had the power to deport an alien who had not committed a criminal offence if it appeared to be in the public interest. Common reasons for such expulsions were failure to register with or report regularly to the police, ignoring work restrictions, and becoming a charge on public funds. Those deported were not permitted to return.

2.11.1 *General sources*
The registers of deportees in HO 372, from 1906 until 1963, usually give name, nationality, date of conviction, offence and whether or not the deportation order was revoked and, if so, when. The volumes are arranged chronologically. The order authorizing an individual's deportation was filed on the alien's personal file.

Other sources for deportees include HO 45 and HO 144. Although most of these files deal mainly with policy and administrative matters, some relate to specific deportation cases.

The National Archives does not hold the records of the courts of summary jurisdiction, which for England and Wales were the Petty, Borough and Quarter Sessions, and magistrates courts. Instead, these are held in local county archives. As Scotland has always had a separate legal system, the relevant Scottish records, including those of courts of summary jurisdiction, are held in Scotland.

2.11.2 *Second World War deportations*
The first two years of the Second World War saw a particularly high number of deportations, with some aliens being temporarily interned in British camps prior to being sent to the colonies and the dominions. Passenger lists survive for merchant vessels leaving British ports for ports outside Europe and the Mediterranean Sea in BT 27 Outwards Passenger Lists. These records can be searched by name and downloaded on *www.ancestorsonboard.com* – see 1.2.4 for further details.

As mentioned above, many ships carrying deported internees were lost at sea by enemy action and these losses resulted in the ending of the policy of deporting internees. BT 334 Registrar General of Shipping and Seamen: Registers and indexes of births, marriages and deaths of passengers and seamen at sea includes returns for aliens. Related records may also be found in HO 213, HO 214 and HO 215. Survivors' reports from lost vessels can be found among the Admiralty war history cases and papers in ADM 1, ADM 116 and ADM 199. A card index, arranged by name of vessel, is located in the Open Reading Room.

Similarly, official inquiries into such losses may be found among the War Cabinet Memoranda in CAB 66.

2.12 Case Studies

2.12.1 *Frank Berni*

Frank Berni was born Francesco Berni at Bardi in Italy on 30 October 1903. He was educated in Italy, migrating to Wales in 1919, where he went to work in a restaurant in Ebbw Vale until 1929, when he went to Exeter and established the Exeter Ice-Cream Company. At the same time, he opened Berni's café in Exeter, in partnership with his father, Louis, and brothers Aldo and Marco. After selling their business he opened, in 1934, a café in High Street, Exeter, followed by another in Plymouth and a café in Bristol in 1938.

After Italy's declaration of war on Britain on 10 June 1940, some 4,000 resident Italians who were known to be members of the Italian Fascist Party and others aged between 16 and 70 who had lived in the UK for less than 20 years were ordered to be interned. Berni was one of them and was arrested under the Defence Act. He was detained in Liverpool prison and spent some time at the Internment camp in Huyton.

On 10 December 1940, he appeared before the Advisory Committee (Italian) to consider appeals against orders of internment. He had earlier been arrested as he was a member of the Italian Fascist Party and had been so since 1923. He became a member because some of his friends had done so and because it enabled him to attend annual dances at the Park Hotel and the Royal Hotel in Cardiff. However, he claimed he had never attended meetings of the Fascio and did not know where their headquarters were in Cardiff. He also said that he never wore the Fascist badge in this country, but that he did when he returned to Italy in the 1920s and 1930s. In a visit in 1933 he was appalled at the brutal methods employed by the Fascists and on his return applied successfully for naturalization, and was granted a British passport in 1935.

Berni denied ever being a member of the Committee of the Cardiff Fascio. He had endeavoured at the beginning of the war to join the Special Constabulary, and later to join the ARP service in Cardiff. He also had no objection to fighting against all the King's enemies, including Italians.

The Committee considered that, far from being a fascist sympathizer, Berni was rooted to this country, that any sympathy he had for Italy had for some time been moribund. As a consequence, the Comittee was more than happy to recommend release from detention.

In 1955, Frank and his brother Aldo founded the first Berni Inn in Bristol. By the end of the 1960s, Berni Inns was one of Britain's fastest-growing public companies. Frank Berni died in 2001 at the age of 96.

Records relating to Frank Berni and his brothers include:

HO 405/2103: Aliens Personal Files: Berni, F Date of Birth: 30.10.1903.

HO 334/135: 1914 British Nationality and Status of Aliens Act: Duplicate Certificates of Naturalization: Certificate AZ 4902 (Frank Berni).

HO 334/136: 1914 British Nationality and Status of Aliens Act: Duplicate Certificates of Naturalization: Certificate AZ 5223 (Aldo Berni).

KV 2/1749: The Security Service: Personal (PF Series) Files, Right Wing Extremists, Marco Berni: Italian.

HO 396/205: Italian Internees Released in UK, A–C, 1940–1.

2.12.2 Ernst Freud

Ernst Freud was born in Vienna in 1890 and was the youngest son of the renowned psychiatrist Sigmund Freud. Ernst and his wife Lucie and three sons Stephen, Lucien, and Clement arrived in the UK on 12 August 1933, as the Nazis rose to power in Germany. Ernst worked as an architect in London and settled at addresses in Lancaster Place and King Henry's Road in Hampstead, and later St. John's Wood Terrace.

After being resident in the UK for five years he was eligible to apply for British naturalization and did so successfully on 30 August 1939. Had he not done so, it is possible that he and his family would face internment for being 'enemy aliens' when war was declared on Germany (and Austria) four days later on 3 September 1939. Sigmund, who had joined them in 1938, also escaped internment as he was over 70 and too old to be considered for internment at that time – he died on 23 September 1939.

Records relating to Ernst Freud include:

MEPO 35/29/4: Metropolitan Police: Aliens Registration Office: Sample Record Cards, Freud, Ernst; Austrian. Date of birth: 6 April 1892.

MEPO 35/29/5: Metropolitan Police: Aliens Registration Office: Sample Record Cards, Freud, Lucie; Austrian. Date of birth: 2 March 1896.

HO 334/135: 1914 British Nationality and Status of Aliens Act: Duplicate Certificates of Naturalization: Certificate BZ 1216 (Ernst Freud), 1939.

FIG. 14 *A letter supporting Frank Berni's release from internment.* HO 405/2103

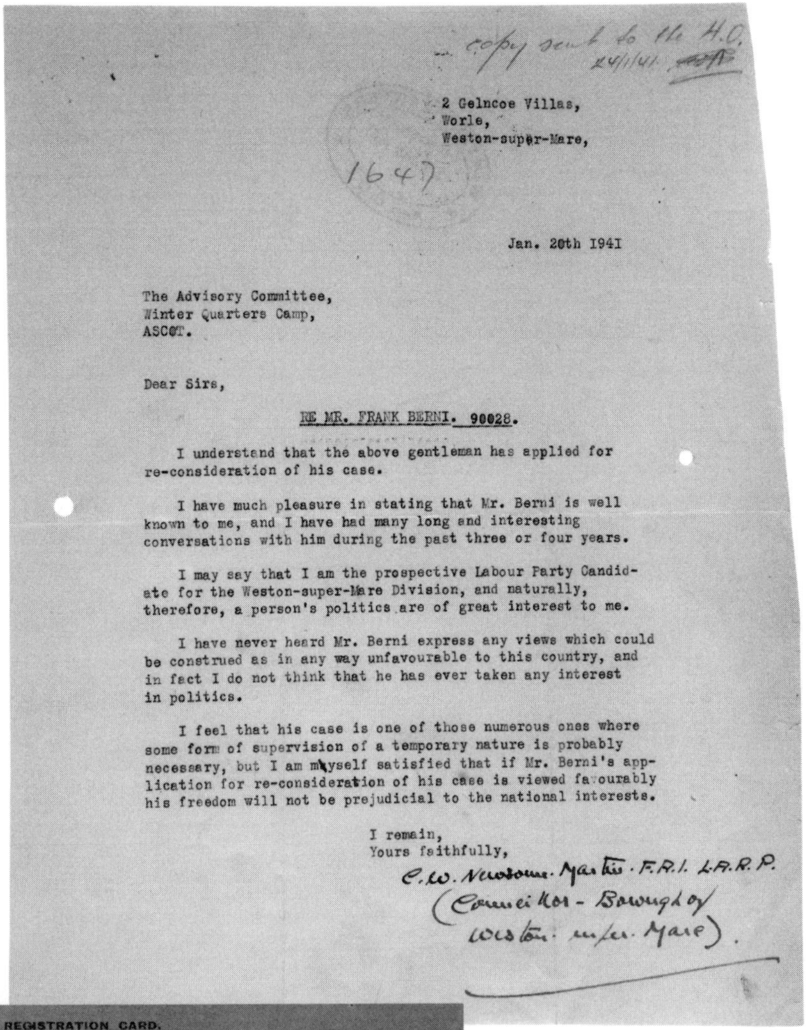

copy sent to the H.O. 24/1/41.

2 Gelncoe Villas,
Worle,
Weston-super-Mare,

1647

Jan. 20th 1941

The Advisory Committee,
Winter Quarters Camp,
ASCOT.

Dear Sirs,

RE MR. FRANK BERNI. 90028.

I understand that the above gentleman has applied for re-consideration of his case.

I have much pleasure in stating that Mr. Berni is well known to me, and I have had many long and interesting conversations with him during the past three or four years.

I may say that I am the prospective Labour Party Candidate for the Weston-super-Mare Division, and naturally, therefore, a person's politics are of great interest to me.

I have never heard Mr. Berni express any views which could be construed as in any way unfavourable to this country, and in fact I do not think that he has ever taken any interest in politics.

I feel that his case is one of those numerous ones where some form of supervision of a temporary nature is probably necessary, but I am myself satisfied that if Mr. Berni's application for re-consideration of his case is viewed favourably his freedom will not be prejudicial to the national interests.

I remain,
Yours faithfully,
C.W. Newsome-Martin. F.R.I. L.A.R.P.
(Councillor - Borough of Weston-super-Mare).

FIG. 15 *Ernst Freud's alien registration card.* MEPO 35/29

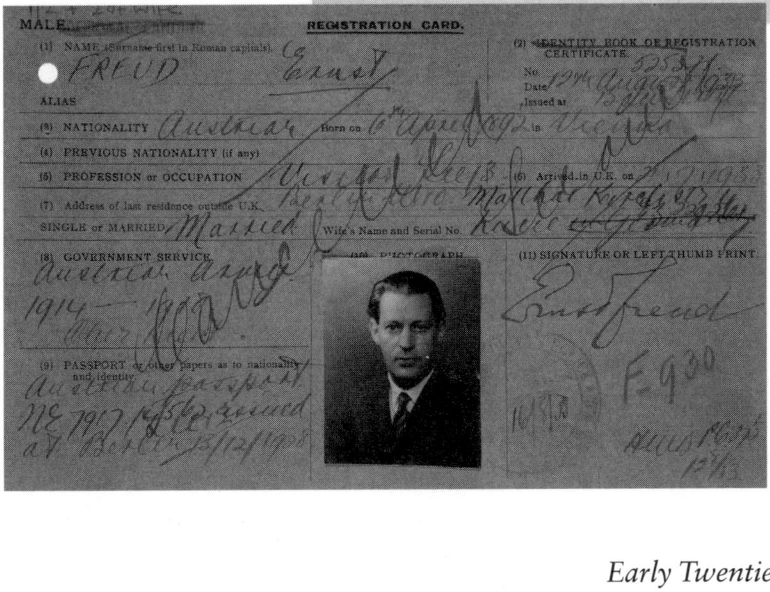

MALE. REGISTRATION CARD.

(1) NAME (Surname first in Roman capitals). FREUD Ernst

(2) IDENTITY BOOK OR REGISTRATION CERTIFICATE. No. Date Issued at

ALIAS

(3) NATIONALITY Austrian Born on 6th April 1892 in Vienna

(4) PREVIOUS NATIONALITY (if any)

(5) PROFESSION or OCCUPATION (6) Arrived in U.K. on

(7) Address of last residence outside U.K.

SINGLE or MARRIED Married Wife's Name and Serial No.

(8) GOVERNMENT SERVICE. Austrian Army 1914–1918

(10) PHOTOGRAPH

(11) SIGNATURE OR LEFT THUMB PRINT. Ernst Freud

(9) PASSPORT or other papers as to nationality and identity. Austrian passport ... issued at Berlin 13/12/1933

F-930

3 MIGRATION AFTER THE SECOND WORLD WAR

Many people who chose to settle in this country in the immediate aftermath of the Second World War had been directly affected by the conflict. Among these were a large portion of the 160,000 Polish servicemen who had fought in Europe with the British forces, and a significant proportion of the many colonists who had been recruited for the same purpose.

Of equal importance in defining the shape of migration in the first decades after the Second World War was the 1948 British Nationality Act. This encouraged tens of thousands of West Indians to migrate to Britain and significantly increased the presence of black communities in Britain. Similarly, it was after the British Nationality Act 1948 that Indian and Pakistani immigrants began to enter the country in significant numbers. The majority of migrants from the Indian sub-continent arrived in Britain in the 1950s and 1960s. Asians expelled from Kenya with British passports settled in the UK in 1967. Similarly, Asians expelled from Uganda with British passports settled here in 1973.

3.1 Polish Resettlement after the Second World War

The Polish soldiers who fought with the British forces in the Second World War were in the main anti-Communist, and less than keen to return to a Poland now dominated by the Soviet Union. They were brought back to the UK as a serving unit; the bulk preferred not to be repatriated to Poland and were allowed to stay in the UK.

3.1.1 Polish Resettlement Corps
In order to ease the transition from a Polish military environment to British civilian life, a satisfactory means of handling demobilization was needed. This took the form of raising, as a corps of the British Army, the Polish Resettlement Corps (PRC), in which Poles were allowed to enlist for the period of their demobilization. Formed in 1946 and disbanded after fulfilling its purpose in 1949, the PRC vetted applicants and discharged them from the Polish armed forces. Wives

and dependent relatives of these men were brought to the UK to join them, bringing the total estimated number of cases to over 200,000.

Records of the Corps are in WO 315 Army Records Centre (Polish Section): Polish Records 1939–50. It should be noted that some of the records are in Polish, although for ease of administration English translations were provided in most cases. The records relate mainly to administrative and policy issues such as organization and disbandment, but a few files are of specific interest to family historians. WO 315/8 consists of PRC army lists and nominal rolls and WO 315/13–14 are records relating to nursing officers in Polish military hospitals and PRC medical officers, dentists and field ambulance officers.

3.1.2 Assistance Board records

The problem of registration, supervision and settlement of the Poles was significant and it imposed a great burden of work not only on the Aliens Branch of the Home Office, but also on all police forces throughout the UK, who needed to maintain alien registers. Information about Poles can be found in the files of the Assistance Board. From 1941 the Board was empowered to grant allowances to persons in need as a direct result of war who would not otherwise have been eligible for unemployment benefit. AST 18 Polish Resettlement contains a selection of files that specifically deal with the problems arising out of the Polish Resettlement Act 1947. The Act placed upon the Assistance Board the responsibility for meeting the needs of Poles and their dependants who had come into this country since September 1939. Before then welfare work for Poles had been undertaken by the Polish Wartime Government in exile in London and then temporarily administered by the Interim Treasury Committee for Polish Questions until the Resettlement Act came into force.

The Act enabled the Assistance Board (renamed the National Assistance Board in 1948) to provide accommodation for those whose resettlement in Britain was going to take some time to achieve. The Board opened a number of hostels, mainly in the south and southeastern regions of England, providing accommodation for over 16,000 Poles. The records in AST 18 Assistance Board and successors: Polish Resettlement, Registered Files (PR Series) reflect the nature of the administrative work of the board and the camps. Related records concerning housing of individual Poles can be found in AST 7/939, 953, 1053–4, 1063, 1254, 1255, 1456–9 and 1909.

3.1.3 The Committee for the Education of Poles

On 1 April 1947, the Minister of Education and the Secretary of State for Scotland established the Committee for the Education of Poles in Great Britain. The Committee, an autonomous body consisting of both British and Polish members, had the responsibility of ensuring that the many thousands of Poles who elected to remain in Britain would be fitted for resettlement here or in former British territories overseas. This largely involved acquiring an adequate knowledge of English and of the British way of life. To encourage this, the purely Polish institutions were eventually dissolved and the children and students educated in equivalent British institutions.

The Committee was wound up on 30 September 1954 with the major part of its task accomplished. The Minister of Education appointed an advisory committee to deal with remaining Polish affairs and a Polish section was established in the Ministry. An Education and Library Committee was also set up at the Polish Research Centre to deal with the Polish libraries and adult education in National Assistance Board Hostels. Both committees were wound up in 1967.

FIG. 16 *T. Brodzki's biographical life sketch and questionnaire.* ED 128/52

My life-sketch.

I am of Polish nationality and Rom.Cath religion. I was born on 24th September 1912 at Pultusk near Warsaw. After the 1914-1918 war my parents moved to Łuck, where I spent my boyhood and was at school. In May 1933 I completed a Secondary School programme of studies at Jarosław near Przemyśl and was matriculated. During the period 18.9.33-18.9.1934 I completed the compulsory military service in the Polish Army (at the Military College - Zambrów, near Warsaw).

Then I was employed for the next 5 years as a bookkeeper and a secretary with the Municipal Council office - Tłumacz, near Stanisławów. In 1937 I married. On 1st January 1938 I was awarded a diploma of a reserve officer.

As an officer of the reserve I was mobilised on 1st September 1939 and took an active part in the Campaign against Germans with the 53 Infantry Regiment. The war ended and I went to join my wife at Dolina near Stanisławów. This part of our Country was occupied by the Red Army.

On 10.4.1940 I was arrested by N.K.V.D (Russian Political Police) and sent to prison at Stanisławów in Poland. On 4.8.1940 transferred to a prison at Melitopol in Russia and then to a prison-camp at Starobielsk.

I was charged with counter-revolutionary activity and condemned to

---

THE ... EDUCATION OF POLES IN GREAT BRITAIN
70-74, Cadogan Square, London, S.W.1

A. IV.

QUESTIONNAIRE.

The Questionnaire should be filled in legibly and all irrelevant questions crossed out. If there is not enough space, separate sheet of paper may be used.

A. 1. Surname /pseudonyms and maiden names should be given/: BRODZKI

Christian names:

2. Christian name:
2. Date and place of birth: 24.9.1912 - PUTTUSK, near Warsaw.

3. Single or married /if married state name of wife or husband/: Married.
Wife: BRODZKA STEFANiA

4. If married state number of children /if any/ and their dates of birth:
1 child: Jerzy - 18.3.1944 - Palestine.

5. Personal documents:

a/ Polish: give number, date and place of issue of passport or other documents certifying nationality.
... gardens, London
S.W.3. 2.7.1948. Certificate of married state.

b/ British: civilian or military: give number, date and place of issue. Civilians should state what status they were given on arrival in Great Britain /family of PFC members, dependents, etc./ and for (i) National Registration what period landing permit was granted.
Identity Card
No: AOA 92626139 Registration Certificate No. A317279
issued at Registration issued at Piccadilly Place - aliens Registra-
Office 27.7.49 tion Office on 26.7.1949.
Watford ... London.

6. Date of departure from Poland: on 13.4.1940

7. Date of arrival in Great Britain: on 22.9.1947

B. 8. Service career: give particulars, with dates of your war service, wounds, degree of disablement.
Have you any British or Polish decorations? If so, which ?

I. Awards granted for service during the war of 1939-45: 1) 1939-45 Star, 2) Italy Star, 3) Defence Medal. 4) War Medal 1939-45.

II. 18.9.33 - 18.9.34 Compulsory Military service in the Polish army - Poland. Military College at Zambrów.
In 1935 } two training period in the Polish army
In 1937 } 6 weeks each. 24 Inf. Reg. Łuck
1.1.1938 awarded a diploma of a reserve officer
In 1938 } 6 weeks training in the Polish army 53 Inf. Reg. Sarny
1.9.1939 - 20.9.1939 active part in the Campaign against Germans 53 Inf. Reg.
17.2.1942 joined the Polish Forces in Russia
17.2.1942 - 11.8.42 Polish Forces Russia
11.8.42 - 26.3.44 ... - Irany, Prague, Palestine, Egypt (2nd Polish corps)
...44 - 28.5.46 2nd Polish Corps active part in the Italian Campaign

56 · *Migration After the Second World War*

The rather lengthily titled series ED 128 Committee for the Education of Poles in Great Britain (Gater Committee) and Ministry of Education, Polish Sections of Awards and External Relation Branches: Polish Resettlement Files records the work of the Board (Ministry from 1943) of Education in respect of Polish resettlement. The series includes awards to successful students as well as questionnaires and biographical life sketches. Previously closed for 75 years, these records (ED 128/42–75) were opened in 1997 following a re-review. The series includes files relating to Polish institutions in Scotland.

3.1.4 *Other sources*

LAB 26 Welfare Matters consists of files relating to general welfare matters and includes records relating to housing estates for Polish workers (LAB 26/187–98 and LAB 26/231).

The majority of aliens arriving between 1940 and 1948 were Poles who eventually applied for naturalization. The series of files in HO 405 will therefore contain a high proportion of applications from ex-PRC men. For information about these records see 2.3.1.

3.2 Hungarian Refugees, 1957

In October 1956 Soviet forces entered Hungary following a year that had begun with a gradual and controlled policy of de-Stalinization and escalated into strong attacks on the Communist regime, culminating in mass demonstrations and uprisings among the Hungarian people. The Soviets employed heavy artillery and bombers against the Hungarian freedom fighters. As the frontier with Austria was, by coincidence, physically open for the first time since 1945 and further, for a while, unguarded, huge numbers of refugees escaped over the borders to safety. Having been given ready assistance in Austria, many thousands found haven in countries in Western Europe and overseas.

A number of case files of Hungarian refugees will appear in HO 405, though these relate mainly to those who had been here as refugees before 1948. See 2.3.1 for information about access to this series. Many Hungarian subjects are included in the sample of police registration cards in MEPO 35 (see 2.3.2).

HO 352/141–9 relates to the admission, residence and employment of Hungarian refugees from the Hungarian revolution. Over 21,000 refugees entered the UK between 1957 and 1958, of whom 6,000 went on to Canada (see 1.2.4 for outgoing passenger lists) and 1,800 chose to return to Hungary. Material relating to the maintenance of Hungarian refugees can be found in AST 7/1621–3. LAB 8/2344 and LAB 8/2371 detail Ministry of Labour administrative and employment arrangements for Hungarian refugees.

FROM VIENNA TO FOREIGN OFFICE

En Clair

FOREIGN OFFICE AND
WHITEHALL DISTRIBUTION

Sir G. Wallinger
No. 344   D. 7.00 p.m. November 22, 1956
November 22, 1956   R. 7.35 p.m. November 22, 1956

IMMEDIATE

My telegram No. 342: Hungarian Refugees.

The Minister was today summoned to the Foreign Ministry and told that 18,000 (repeat 18,000) refugees had crossed the border in the last thirty hours. Many of them had to swim or wade through rivers and marshes in ten degrees of frost. Others were wounded. Everything was breaking down and if the influx were to continue (as was likely) the situation would soon be catastrophic. The number of refugees still in Austria was over 50,000.

2.   The Austrian representatives abroad and foreign representatives here were being asked to represent to foreign governments the appalling proportions which this problem has now assumed. The Austrian Government thought it essential that the whole of Western Europe should now become a "first asylum" area to which refugees could be moved in large numbers at once. Foreign railway administrations are being urged to send in trains for this purpose, since much Austrian rolling stock is already abroad with refugees. Her Majesty's Government are asked to help in every way possible and in particular to increase the quota and speed of intake into the United Kingdom and to use their influence with appropriate Commonwealth Governments so that the largest possible numbers of refugees may reach those countries through the United Kingdom. Refugees now coming in are stated to be good potential immigrants with a high proportion of young people who feared deportation.

3.   The American and Swedish quotas have now been tripled, the Netherlands and Swedish [sic] quotas have been doubled and the German quota is likely to be doubled.

ADVANCE COPIES:
Private Secretary
Sir I. Kirkpatrick
Mr. Wright
Head of General Department
Head of News Department
Resident Clerk

FIG. 17 *A Foreign Office telegram sent in the aftermath of the 1956 Hungarian revolution.*
HO 352/141

3.3 The British Nationality Act, 1948

This applied to British subjects or citizens of Ireland, the Channel Islands, the Isle of Man, any colony or protectorate and certain protected states. Under the Act, certificates of British nationality could be issued to subjects of any British colony or protectorate on application, and Home Office copies of these records can be found in the series of records HO 334. In theory, this applied to some 800 million people when all of Britain's possessions overseas were taken into consideration. In reality, the numbers were relatively small. See section 6.7.3 for registration of British citizenship documents 1948–87.

The Act was in part a response to a report from a working party the British government had set up to tackle the problem of the continuing shortage of unskilled labour. The working party had aimed to solve the problem by making use of unemployed workers from the British colonies, especially those from the West Indies. For example, the population of Jamaica was expanding at a rate that could not easily be contained by the economy. Many West Indians stayed in Britain after wartime service and those that returned home often found the conditions and opportunities there poor and found it difficult to readjust to such limitations.

In Britain, however, colonial workers were now facing prejudice from employers. The working party was concerned about the discrimination that black workers would face in Britain and the difficulties involved in assimilating them. It therefore recommended no large-scale immigration of male colonial workers. The working party preferred European volunteer workers, as they were subject to strict labour controls and could be prosecuted or deported if they broke their conditions of recruitment. The working party was more sympathetic to the recruitment of female colonial workers, noting the serious labour shortages in domestic employment, the health service and textile industries. The findings of this working party can be found in LAB 26/226.

3.4 Lists of Migrants from the Colonies

The only lists of migrants from the colonies are the inwards passenger lists in BT 26, which survive up to and including 1960; they are available online to search and download (for a fee) at *www.ancestry.co.uk*. These give the names of all passengers arriving in the UK where the ship's voyage began at a port outside Europe and the Mediterranean Sea. Many of the passenger lists in BT 26 for voyages that began in the West Indies or southeast Asia between 1948 and 1960 have been digitized and indexed by name on the free website Moving Here (*www.movinghere.org.uk*). Such lists include that for the *Empire Windrush*, which was arguably the first ship to bring significant numbers of West Indian workers to London in 1948 (Fig. 19).

Researchers should be aware that large numbers of those who came to Britain from the Indian sub-continent came by aircraft or by train, entering Victoria, via Calais and Dover, after disembarking from their ships on the Continent in such ports as Marseilles, Genoa and Vigo. The National Archives does not hold arrival passenger lists for voyages that began at European ports or lists of arrivals by air. See 1.1.3 for further details.

3.4.1 Colonial records

Individual colonies set up schemes and committees to deal with the administration of emigration to the United Kingdom. Records of general migration schemes may be found among the series CO 323. Correspondence relating to schemes in specific colonies may be found under relevant CO (Colonial Office) correspondence series, arranged by name of colony. Papers include schemes set up to deal with migration from the colonies, particularly with regards to the employment, recruitment and welfare of specific categories of workers. These series also include studies of migration movements and reports on how easily migrants from the colonies settled in the UK.

The series DO 35 Dominions Office and Commonwealth Relations Office: Original Correspondence and DO 175 General and Migration Records include files relating to measures for control of migration from the colonies during the 1950s. Later records (from 1967) can be found in FCO 50 Foreign and Commonwealth Office: General and Migration Department.

3.4.2 Central government and colonial immigration

CAB 128 Cabinet Minutes and CAB 129 Cabinet Memoranda include references to reviews of colonial immigration, and paper copies of the records are available in the Open Reading Room. Cabinet Committees were set up specifically to look at the immigration of British subjects into the United Kingdom. CAB 130/61 consists of papers relating to concerns that the increase in immigrants from dependent territories to Britain since 1945 was swelling the numbers of unemployed workers. The relevant committee considered introducing new laws to govern the entry of aliens, as well as measures that could be adopted to control this trend and any policy issues this might involve. Most of the migrants came from West Africa, the West Indies, Somaliland, Aden and the Mediterranean colonies.

Of particular interest are the Cabinet Secretary's Notebooks in CAB 195. Recently released, these records consist of longhand notebooks of Cabinet meetings and some other meetings of ministers during the period 1942–56 (though later records will be made available in due course). The notebooks provide more detailed accounts of the meetings than appear in the printed records.

As there was then no central government mechanism to govern and manage colonial immigration, the Home Office used the data on which it could accurately estimate annual net colonial immigration. Shipping and air transport passenger lists did not, for example, distinguish reliably between intending migrants and tourists. For the years 1955–60, the Home Office estimated a net influx of 160,000 West Indian migrants, compared with 33,000 from India and 17,000 from Pakistan.

Home Office general files relating to establishment matters, policy, disturbances and casework on a variety of immigration and aliens issues can be found in HO 213, HO 325, HO 352, HO 355, HO 367 and HO 394.

Ministry of Labour files relating to the employment, welfare and training of the new arrivals can be found in the series LAB 8, LAB 13 and LAB 26. These papers include reports and papers on the Commonwealth Immigrants Act 1962 (see 3.6).

Metropolitan Police files relating to attitudes towards colonial migrants, the integration of colonial migrants into local communities and issues relating to law and order and disturbances can be found in MEPO 2. Cases investigated by the Race Relations Board are in CK 2.

3.5 Establishing Roots

According to the 1961 census there were some 50,000 Muslims in Britain and seven places of worship, 16,000 Sikhs with three places of worship and 30,000 Hindus with only one place of worship. One particularly interesting aspect of the records held at the National Archives

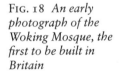

FIG. 18 *An early photograph of the Woking Mosque, the first to be built in Britain*

is the light cast on how new arrivals addressed the need to establish proper religious houses. Among these are, for example, correspondence relating to proposals to establish a Hindu temple and India Cultural Centre in London in DO 163/83. The National Archives also holds records relating to the construction of the Regent's Park Mosque. George VI presented its site to the Muslim authorities in Britain in 1944, nearly 50 years after the first British mosque had been built in Woking.

Correspondence relating to the acquisition of the Regent's Park site can be found in WORK 16/1575-6 for the period 1940–55, while that regarding the mosque's erection can be found in WORK 16/2236-7 for the period 1963–71. Further documents relating to the mosque and the competition to design it can be found in CRES 35/4909 and 5193, CRES 57/194 and IF 6/123. Other documents are potentially instructive in illustrating the conflicts that have arisen around religious practice in a new country. These include MEPO 28/6 which details the regulations surrounding the scattering of the cremated remains of Sikhs and Hindus on inland waterways and HO 387/1448, which covers the Metropolitan Police's debate on the wearing of turbans by Sikh officers.

Researchers could consider investigating the records of associations and societies, while community newspapers and magazines can also prove valuable sources of information. You should also explore the Access to Archives website at *www.a2a.org.uk* along with the appropriate local county record office websites. The Moving Here website at *www.movinghere.org.uk/galleries/roots/asian/asian.htm* also provides useful guidance on exploring South Asian family history.

3.6   The Commonwealth Immigrants Act 1962

This Act was introduced after more than a decade of mounting public pressure for some restriction of immigration from the British colonies. The fear that new restrictive legislation was about to be implemented drew in larger numbers of migrants from the Caribbean in 1961 and 1962. The Commonwealth Immigrants Bill, which passed through the Commons in July 1962, required all Commonwealth citizens seeking employment in Britain to qualify for a voucher. Particular emphasis was laid on the control of unskilled workers, and those with passports not issued in Britain were obliged to hold a work permit to secure entry. After 1962 there was never again to be a return to the unrestricted policies of the post-war years. Indeed, the controls were further tightened by the Commonwealth Immigrants Act 1968. Potential immigrants were now required to prove that they themselves had been born in the United Kingdom, or that their parents or grandparents had been.

The Commonwealth Relations Office also dealt with issues relating to immigration to Britain and these can be found in DO 35, DO 175, and FCO 50.

Vouchers for the employment of Commonwealth citizens were introduced under the Commonwealth Immigrants Acts 1962 and 1968. The vouchers were issued in two categories: Category A for Commonwealth citizens with a definite offer of a job, and Category B for those who held certain specified professional qualifications. Application for a Category A voucher was made by the prospective employer. Except for Malta and the Dependent Territories, Category B vouchers were issued for those holding professional qualifications and managerial and executive staff; skilled craftsmen and experienced teachers; specialized clerical and secretarial staff; and those coming for work which, in the opinion of the Secretary of State for Employment, was of substantial economic and social value to the United Kingdom.

Category A vouchers were not issued if the vacancy offered could be filled by resident labour. Special arrangements existed for the admission, without vouchers, of doctors and dentists. Only a limited number of vouchers were issued annually, based on fixed quotas for the various countries of the Commonwealth. LAB 42 consists of specimen applications. All pieces in this series are open to public inspection following a re-review in 1998 and are arranged by name of applicant.

The issue of vouchers was brought to an end by the Immigration Act 1971, which came into force on 1 January 1973. The effect of this Act was to bring Commonwealth citizens in line with citizens of foreign

FIG. 19 *Passengers arriving on the* Empire Windrush *in 1948*

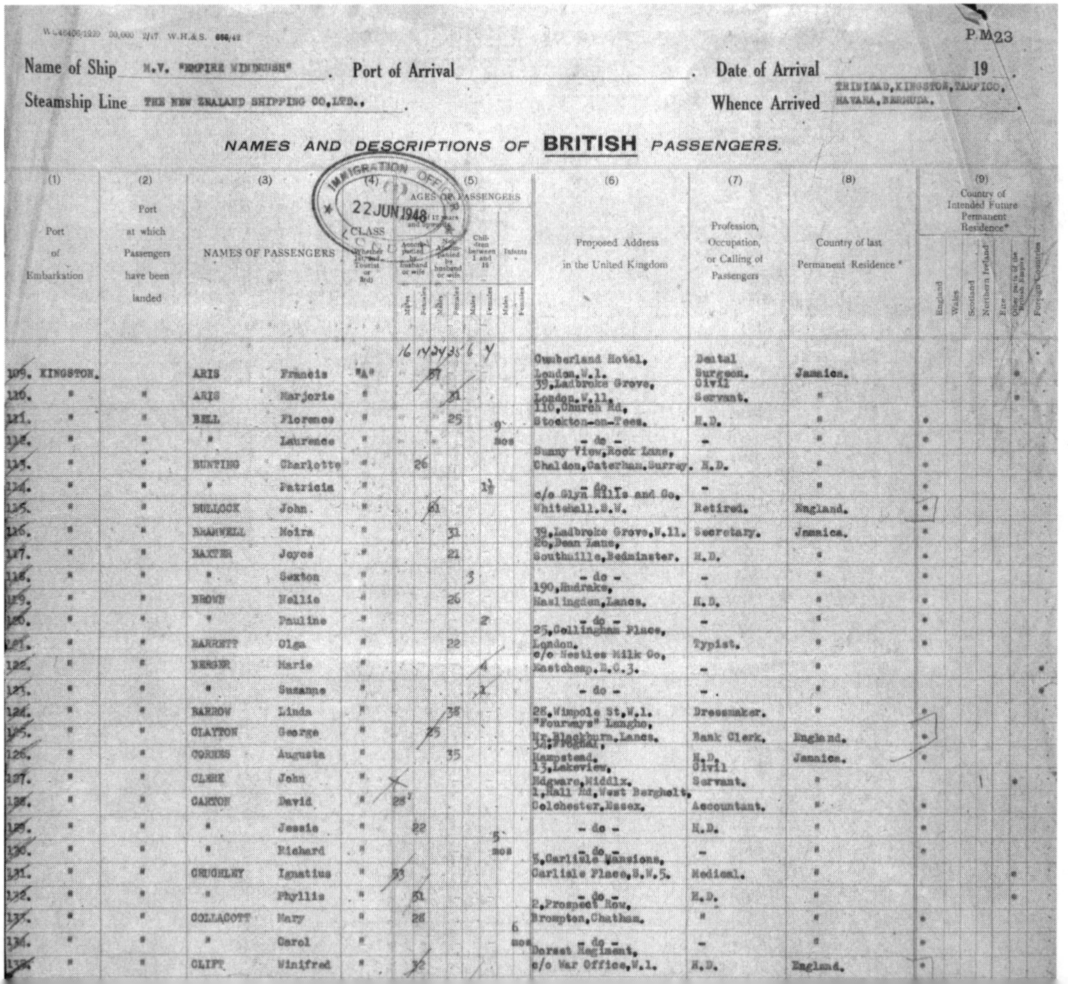

W.48406/1920 30,000 2/47 W.H.&S. 666/42 P.M.23

Name of Ship M.V. "EMPIRE WINDRUSH". Port of Arrival . Date of Arrival 19 .

Steamship Line THE NEW ZEALAND SHIPPING CO, LTD., . Whence Arrived TRINIDAD, KINGSTON, TAMPICO, HAVANA, BERMUDA.

NAMES AND DESCRIPTIONS OF **BRITISH** PASSENGERS.

IMMIGRATION OFFICE 22 JUN 1948

	(1) Port of Embarkation	(2) Port at which Passengers have been landed	(3) Names of Passengers		(4) Class	(5) Ages of Passengers	(6) Proposed Address in the United Kingdom	(7) Profession, Occupation, or Calling of Passengers	(8) Country of last Permanent Residence*	(9) Country of Intended Future Permanent Residence*: England	Other parts of the British Empire	Foreign Countries
						16 1/24 35 6 Y						
109.	KINGSTON.		ARIS	Francis	"A"	57	Cumberland Hotel, London, W.1.	Dental Surgeon.	Jamaica.		•	
110.	"	"	ARIS	Marjorie	"	31	39, Ladbroke Grove, London, W.11.	Civil Servant.	"		•	
111.	"	"	BELL	Florence	"	25	110, Church Rd, Stockton-on-Tees.	H.D.	"	•		
112.	"	"	"	Laurence	"	9 mos	- do -	-	"	•		
113.	"	"	BUNTING	Charlotte	"	26	Sunny View, Rock Lane, Chaldon, Caterham, Surrey.	H.D.	"	•		
114.	"	"	"	Patricia	"	1½	- do -	-	"	•		
115.	"	"	BULLOCK	John	"	61	c/o Glyn Mills and Co, Whitehall, S.W.	Retired.	England.	•		
116.	"	"	BRAMWELL	Moira	"	31	39, Ladbroke Grove, W.11.	Secretary.	Jamaica.	•		
117.	"	"	BAXTER	Joyce	"	21	26, Dean Lane, Southville, Bedminster.	H.D.	"	•		
118.	"	"	"	Sexton	"	3	- do -	-	"	•		
119.	"	"	BROWN	Nellie	"	26	190, Endrake, Haslingden, Lancs.	H.D.	"	•		
120.	"	"	"	Pauline	"	2	- do -	-	"	•		
121.	"	"	BARRETT	Olga	"	22	25, Collingham Place, London.	Typist.	"	•		
122.	"	"	BERGER	Marie	"	4	c/o Nestles Milk Co, Eastcheap, E.C.3.	-	"			•
123.	"	"	"	Suzanne	"	1	- do -	-	"			•
124.	"	"	BARROW	Linda	"	38	28, Wimpole St, W.1.	Dressmaker.	"	•		
125.	"	"	CLAYTON	George	"	25	"Fourways" Langho, Nr. Blackburn, Lancs.	Bank Clerk.	England.	•		
126.	"	"	CORNES	Augusta	"	35	3?, Frognal, Hampstead.	H.D.	Jamaica.	•		
127.	"	"	CLERK	John	"		13, Lakeview, Edgware, Middlx.	Civil Servant.	"		•	
128.	"	"	CARTON	David	"	28	1, Hall Rd, West Bergholt, Colchester, Essex.	Accountant.	"	•		
129.	"	"	"	Jessie	"	22	- do -	H.D.	"	•		
130.	"	"	"	Richard	"	5 mos	- do -	-	"	•		
131.	"	"	CRUGHLEY	Ignatius	"	53	5, Carlisle Mansions, Carlisle Place, S.W.5.	Medical.	"		•	
132.	"	"	"	Phyllis	"	51	- do -	H.D.	"		•	
133.	"	"	COLLACOTT	Mary	"	28	2, Prospect Row, Brompton, Chatham.	"	"	•		
134.	"	"	"	Carol	"	6 mos	- do -	-	"	•		
135.	"	"	CLIFT	Winifred	"	32	Dorset Regiment, c/o War Office, W.1.	H.D.	England.	•		

countries, in so far as employment was concerned, which meant that Commonwealth citizens had to have a prospective employer in order to come to this country to work.

LAB 48 contains specimen application's from aliens, 1968 to 1972, and from 1973 onwards, from both aliens and Commonwealth citizens. The majority of these records are open to public inspection following a re-review in 1998.

3.7 Expulsions from Uganda and Kenya

On 4 August 1972 President Idi Amin decreed the expulsion of UK passport holders from Uganda within 90 days. Those affected were largely of Asian origin. The Uganda Resettlement Board was appointed by the Home Secretary to assist UK passport holders and their dependants who were ordinarily resident in Uganda on that date. Its remit extended to the children of any such persons born since then.

The first Asian immigrants from Uganda arrived in the UK by air on 18 September. By the end of the year, some 25,000 had entered the country. The reception of expelled persons in the UK was undertaken with the help of voluntary organizations and local authorities. Temporary accommodation was provided, mainly in resettlement centres. Expelled persons were discouraged from going to areas where services were particularly under stress and where houses were unlikely to be available. Problems were mainly resolved by local authorities and voluntary organizations who were used to meeting similar needs of the indigenous population.

HO 289 contains minutes and papers of the Uganda Resettlement Board. The Board's first meeting was held on 30 August 1972. Its interim report was published in May 1973 and its final report in April 1974.

Further sources relating to this expulsion can be found in records of the Foreign and Commonwealth Office, specifically FCO 31/1375 –1401, 1441–8, FCO 50/396–416, FCO 53/278–80 and FCO 89/9–10. There are also Prime Minister's Office correspondence in PREM 15/1727 and 1818 and Department of Education files in ED 269/14 and ED 233/11.

Those fleeing Uganda followed in the footsteps of Asians who began travelling to Britain in 1967 to escape the repressive regime in Kenya. Records relating to these immigrants can be found in LAB 8/3409, HO 344/49 and the series FCO 47 and FCO 50, though these are mainly policy files, with few if any lists of individuals.

4 FOUR CENTURIES OF REFUGEES

Refugees were defined by the League of Nations in 1926 as individuals with a national origin who no longer enjoy the protection of that national government and have not yet acquired another nationality. While many people might think of the phenomenon as a modern one, groups of refugees have been seeking safety here since the sixteenth century. Many of those who sought refuge chose to remain, establishing their own communities which would maintain their distinct character for years to come. At the same time members of these communities sought naturalization or were made denizens, generating documents of great interest to family historians. See chapters 5 and 6 for more information on these processes.

4.1 The Reformation and Religious Refugees

The sixteenth century saw the Reformation in Germany and an influx of Protestant refugees until Henry VIII's break with Rome. Although their numbers were small to begin with, they were not particularly welcome. Politically, aliens were seen to be a menace to the realm, especially when diplomatic relations with other powers were strained or when war broke out. In one area, however, immigration was viewed in a more positive light. Henry VIII favoured certain groups of skilled labourers, such as ordnance workers, gunners and armourers from France, Germany and the Low Countries, settling in England. Mathematical practitioners, instrument makers and surveyors were encouraged to enter the king's employment and many of these were made denizens for this purpose. See chapter 5 for material relating to early denization records.

There were other immigrants too, such as Dutch tapestry-makers, Flemish weavers, and glaziers from France and the Low Countries. They often settled in the liberties and precincts of the monasteries where they had freedom from the jurisdiction of the city authorities. The growing numbers led to an Act in 1523 (14/15 Hen. VIII c. 2), regulating stranger craftsmen, and a further Act in 1529 (21 Hen. VIII c. 16) to control their activities and regulate their relationships with the

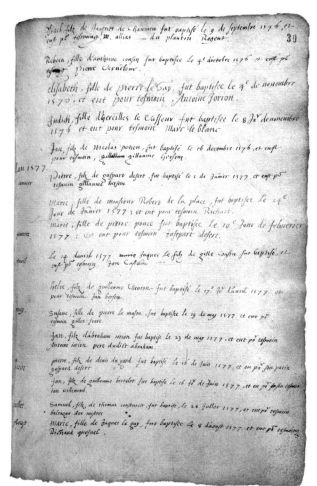

FIG. 20 *A register of baptisms from the Walloon church of St. Julian, Southampton.* RG 4/4600

city companies. A third Act of 1540 (32 Hen. VIII c. 16) strengthened the law relating to stranger denizens and patents of denization. Following this legislation many of the foreign workmen settled in England took oaths of loyalty as required by the Act of 1529 and paid the necessary fees to obtain patents of denization.

In 1550 Edward VI granted by letters patent the use of the former Austin Friars Church to the German refugees and other strangers. A Pole, John a'Lasco, was to be their superintendent. Initially the church was used by German, Dutch and French congregations. The congregation was dispersed during the reign of Mary, but was restored after Elizabeth came to the throne, under the care of the Bishop of London. The Belgian Walloons and French-speaking congregation obtained the lease of St Anthony's Church in Threadneedle Street. You can find registers of baptisms, burials and marriages conducted at this church at *www.bmd registers.co.uk*.

Other communities opened their own churches. One of the earliest nonconformist congregations in England was a foreign community of Walloons in Southampton. A register of baptisms survives, again at *www.bmdregisters.co.uk*, which is free to search (by name and type of event – baptism, marriage and burial) and to download at the National Archives. In 1567, Southampton was willing to admit Dutch settlers who had fled persecution in their own country (SP 12/43 no. 16, f. 41).

Meanwhile, protestants from the Low Countries, who had been driven from their homeland by the harsh rule of Spain, petitioned the queen to be allowed to settle in England and carry on their occupations. See SP 12/43 no. 29, ff. 66v–68v.

4.2 The Huguenots

The Huguenots were French Protestant refugees, who began to flee to England from the mid-sixteenth century onwards, especially after the massacre of St Bartholomew's Eve in 1572 and until the issuing of the

Edict of Nantes in 1598 granted them tolerance in France. With its revocation in 1685, large numbers of Huguenots again fled and settled in England. Their main settlements were in London, Norwich, Canterbury, Southampton, Rye, Sandwich, Colchester, Bristol and Plymouth. Many records and studies of the Huguenots have been published by the Huguenot Library, University College, Gower Street, London, WC1E 6BT. Their website *www.huguenotsociety.org.uk* provides guidance for researchers who think they may have Huguenot ancestry.

4.2.1 State Papers and Privy Council records

State Papers should be consulted for material on the Huguenots, particularly SP 12 State Papers Domestic, Elizabeth I and, later, SP 31 State Papers Domestic, James II and SP 32 State Papers Domestic, William and Mary. These are calendared in the *Calendar of State Papers, Domestic Series*. SP 44 State Papers: Entry Books contains applications for denization, including many for French Protestants. (SP 44/67, in particular, covers the period 1678 to 1688.)

PC 2 Privy Council: Registers contains minutes of proceedings, orders, reports, etc. The volumes are fully indexed and Huguenots should be looked for under the heading French Protestants. From 1670 onwards it is also worth consulting PC 4 Minutes and Associated Papers which contains indexed volumes of minute books, many relating to French Protestants.

4.2.2 Naturalization of foreign Protestants

Under a statute of 1708 for the Naturalization of Foreign Protestants (7 Anne c. 5) all Protestant refugees (mainly Huguenots) who took the oaths of allegiance and supremacy in a court of law, and who could produce a sacrament certificate, were deemed to have been naturalized, without the need for individual Acts of Parliament.

In passing the Act, Parliament recognized the opportunity for increasing wealth by simplifying the process of naturalization. The Act enabled aliens to be declared natives on taking the oaths of allegiance and signing the declaration in the Courts of England, Scotland or the Quarter Sessions. They also needed to produce proof that they had taken the Sacrament in some Protestant or reformed congregation within the United Kingdom in the past three months. The Act was repealed in 1710, apart from one clause which allowed for children born abroad of natural-born subjects to be taken to be natural-born subjects themselves. You can find the oath roll for oaths taken by aliens in the court of the Exchequer from 1709 to 1711 at E 169/86. Copies of the sacrament certificates of those naturalized under the statute are in E 196/10 (Fig. 21). This has been published by the Huguenot Society, vol. xxxv (1932), pp. 11–33, and is available at the National Archives.

Series KB 24 and E 169/86 include lists of foreign Protestants who, under the Act of 7 Anne c. 5 in 1708 were deemed to have become naturalized by taking the oaths of allegiance and supremacy in the open court. These records survive for the period 1708–11. These have also been published by the Huguenot Society, vol. xxvii (1923), pp. 72–107, again available at the National Archives. Sacrament certificates presented at the court of Chancery may be found in C 224, but there are gaps. Oaths taken locally at Quarter Sessions should be looked for locally among Quarter Sessions records in county record offices. See chapters 5 and 6 further information on citizenship records.

FIG. 21 *Sacrament certificate for Marc Anthony Bruyet.* E 196/10

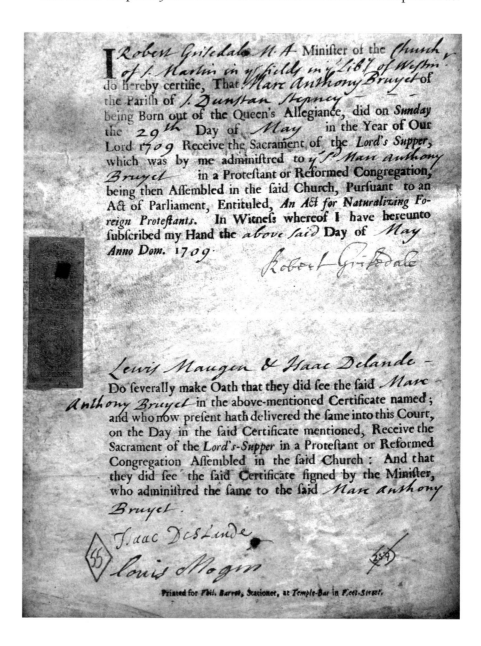

4.2.3 The French Committee

National collections were made for the French Protestant refugees in 1681, 1686, 1688 and 1694. Additional money was given by the Crown and, later, Parliamentary grants. The French Committee administered these grants of money for the relief of French refugees. Surviving records of this body are held by the Huguenot Library, University College, London.

The French Protestant Church of London has its own library and holds its own registers and other records. The London Metropolitan Archives, 40 Northampton Road, London, EC1R OHB has a collection of Huguenot Society publications and collections of material on Huguenot businesses and individuals.

4.2.4 Palatinate Refugees

In 1709 over 6,600 German refugees from the Rhineland Palatinate and southwest Germany found a temporary home in London. Most were planning to settle as colonists in North America, but some abandoned this idea and settled in Ireland, in Limerick and Kerry, subsidized by the Irish government. Some settled in the Scilly Isles, and others found employment in the coal mines of the north of England. Lists of some of these refugees arriving in London can be found in T 1/119 giving names of individuals and the number of dependants.

4.3 French Émigrés, 1789–1815

An influx of French refugees between 1789 and 1814, as a result of the revolution and Napoleonic wars, produced much government concern and documentation, resulting in the Aliens Act 1793 (see 1.1.1 for further information). The series T 50/57–75 contains some material on French ships and expenses of refugees.

4.3.1 Bouillon Papers

The Bouillon Papers in HO 69 are a collection of papers and letters to Philippe d'Auvergne, Prince de Bouillon, as 'Administrateur des Secours Accordes aux Emigres'. From 1794 to 1815 Bouillon served as the senior naval officer in Jersey defending the Channel Islands, gathering intelligence and supporting French royalist refugees who had fled to Jersey. He was aided by the British government, which provided money for the support of the refugees. The most relevant papers relating to Émigrés are in HO 69/33–8, which includes letters and memorials from intending immigrants.

Other papers of the Prince de Bouillon concerning military matters and the defence of the Channel Islands can be found in FO 95 and WO 1. There are two registers of refugees in Jersey, arranged chronologically from 1793 to 1796 (FO 95/602–03). Privy Council records also contain some of his papers (PC 1/115–22, 134–5 and 4490–516). A detailed list of these papers can be found in the non-standard finding aids, which are arranged in series order on the open shelves in the Open Reading Room.

4.3.2 *Calonne Papers*
Charles Alexandre de Calonne was Controller General of France 1783–7, before living in exile in England. After his death his papers were seized by the British government, which subsequently purchased them from his son. These papers mainly relate to commercial and political matters and can be found in Foreign Office (FO 95/630–53) and Privy Council records (PC 1/123–33 and 4517). A detailed list can be found with the Bouillon list in the Open Reading Room.

4.3.3 *French Refugee and Relief Committee*
The Treasury set up the French Refugee and Relief Committee in 1792. Its records are in the series T 93 French Refugee and Relief Committee: Records covering the period 1792 to 1823. They contain lists of names of those receiving pensions. There are accounts, letter books, memorials and pension lists for the relief of laity and clergy. The series also includes accounts and vouchers for French Protestant refugees from 1813 to 1828. Account books relating to this fund for Protestants for the years 1794 to 1836 are in the British Library (ref. Egerton Mss. 2728–832).

4.4 Nineteenth-Century Refugees

In terms of numbers the largest groups of refugees in the nineteenth century were the Irish, together with Polish (and Russian) Jews fleeing the pogroms in the Russian Empire. Also present were Spanish refugees escaping the Carlist Wars. Foreign refugees can be traced from the middle of the century alongside other migrants in general sources such as the census returns (see chapter 9) and naturalization records (see chapter 6).

4.4.1 *Polish and Spanish refugees*
Allowances paid to Polish refugees and distressed Spaniards can be found in PMG 53/2–8 and PMG 53/1–9 respectively. The registers are individually indexed and cover the period 1860 to 1899. The allowances ceased on the death of the last surviving Polish pensioner in 1899. There are also pay lists for the Poles from 1841 to 1856 (T 50/81–97). The allowances ceased on the death of the last Spanish pensioner in 1909.

5 MOVEMENTS BEFORE 1800

The foreign community in England during the medieval period came into being largely through the growth of trade between England and her neighbours. Amongst the early communities of migrants were, however, a number of noteworthy groups including Jewish and black settlers, the former expelled in its entirety in 1290 before formally being allowed to resettle from 1656. Though some of the records mentioned here are quite old, some such as those relating to denization and naturalization can contain a surprising amount of information.

5.1 Alien Merchants and Immigrants in the Medieval Period

The development of trade in the fourteenth century resulted in aliens becoming some of the most important merchants in England. The policy of Edward III and Richard II was one of encouraging trade by granting alien merchants the freedom to trade. Some records of the Italian bankers to the Crown can be found in c 47, Chancery Miscellanea. In 1350 Edward III had set aside the privileges of London and other boroughs so that all merchants of friendly countries could sell their wares freely, wholesale or retail, in spite of franchises (Parliament Rolls or *Rotuli Parliamentorum ii.232*). This appears to have been a temporary measure, possibly as a result of the Black Death, and London soon regained its privileges.

A proclamation was made in 1378 that foreign merchants could come to England under the king's protection and trade wholesale and retail in victuals, spices, fruit, furs and all kinds of small goods (*Rot. Parl. iii.47*). They were restricted to dealing wholesale in wine and great merchandise, such as cloth and linen, retail dealing in such goods being reserved to the native burgesses of the towns and the guilds merchant.

5.2 Taxation and Customs Records

The inquests, assessments and accounts in the series E 179 are a potentially useful resource for those looking for records relating to early immigrants. Here you can find records relating to the alien subsidy, which was introduced in the fifteenth century. Candidates for this tax included alien householders and (from 1449) alien merchants and their clerks. Researchers should be aware, however, that the value of the returns is limited because of widespread evasion and the difficulty of collecting the tax. It is also true that some groups were not held liable. These included members of religious orders, Welshmen, children under 12 years old and some denizens (see 5.3). Irishmen and Channel Islanders were also made exempt in 1442, as were certain groups of foreign merchants in 1483 and 1487.

The alien subsidy ceased to be granted as a separate tax in 1512 but the tax on aliens was included in the grants of lay subsidies made in the sixteenth and early seventeenth centuries. The returns are most numerous for 1440 and 1483–4 .

The E 179 database accessible through the National Archives website *www.nationalarchives.gov.uk/e179/search.asp* provides detailed descriptions of all 27,000 items and can be searched by places occurring in the documents, the grant of taxation to which the document relates, date of document and type of document. Each piece or item within the E 179 series has a database record which gives a description of the physical appearance of the document, the administrative purpose for which the document was created, the date on which it was produced, the tax or taxes to which it relates, and a list of the place-name headings contained within it.

In 1290, the Exchequer sent out instructions for the customs officers of each port to enter the record of dues collected for each port. The surviving account rolls are to be found in E 122 Particulars of Customs' Accounts. These record: the names of ships using the port; the names of the masters; dates of arrival or departure and the names of the merchants in whose names the goods were shipped (annotated to denote whether denizen, alien or Hanse); each item of customable cargo, often with its value; and, in the case of the collectors' accounts, the amount payable. This class also contains Exchequer type rolls drawn up after the audit of the accounts and before their enrolment. Accounts which survive in this form often give less information than the rolls of particulars. The list of E 122 is arranged by port, and then by date of account. Some of these accounts have been printed: E.M. Carus-Wilson (ed.), *The Overseas Trade of Bristol in the Later Middle Ages* (1937); D.M. Daren (ed.), *The Making of King's Lynn: A Documentary Survey* (1984); W. Childs (ed.), *The Customs' Accounts of Hull 1453–1490* (1986); H.S. Cobb (ed.), *The Overseas Trade of London 1480–1* (1990).

The enrolled accounts on the E 372 Pipe Rolls and the E 352 Chancellor's Rolls, and from 1323 the E 356 Enrolled Customs' Accounts, do not name individual merchants unless they were exempt from payment. The Exchequer Memoranda Rolls (E 159 and E 368) include cases of merchants who attempted to defraud the customs revenue.

Later records of duties paid at particular ports are in E 190 Port Books from 1565 to 1799. Many books are in poor condition and some do not survive. There are no books for London between 1697 and 1799. See 1.3.1 for more information.

5.3 Denization, Naturalization and Citizenship

From medieval times, if you were born within the king's allegiance you were his subject. At this point in history, the concepts of state and statehood and nationality were not clearly defined. The king had subjects in England who were English, but he also had possessions in France and subjects who were French.

With the loss of territories on the continent in the reign of Edward III, those born outside the king's allegiance were a stranger, or an alien owing allegiance to another prince. The distinction between natural-born English subjects and aliens was first made in 1335 with the first piece of citizenship legislation (Act 9 Edw. III c. 1). This not only defined an alien as being a person of a foreign nation or allegiance but also ordered aliens residing in England to pay a double rate of taxation. This had the dual effect of raising extra revenue for the Crown and of allowing the Crown some control of aliens in England.

Aliens resident in England could try to improve their position and acquire the privileges of natural-born citizens by obtaining letters of denizen granted by the Crown. Alternatively they could obtain a private act of naturalization by introducing a private bill into Parliament. Denization conferred privileges, including the right to buy but not inherit land. These privileges would be passed on to children born after the grant, but not to any born before. In making his grants of denization by letters patent the king could include whatever stipulations he desired, such as whether or not a grantee would be liable to pay native or alien customs rates. Naturalization conferred a position in all respects similar to that of a natural-born citizen once enacted.

The distinction between denization by letters patent of the king and naturalization by Act of Parliament did not at first exist and took time to evolve. Petitions could be made to Parliament, and Parliament would agree to letters patent being issued. Conversely, grants by letters patent could be confirmed by Act of Parliament.

The first instance of a distinction is in the case of Henry Hansforth in 1431, when Parliament passed a bill giving him the full rights of a native subject (Fig. 22). The king amended the provisions so that he would pay customs as would a stranger, that is, a foreigner. This development helps to explain the subsequent emergence, during the Tudor period, of two main distinctions between denization and naturalization – the granter and the rights conferred. This dual system continued after the Tudor period. In the seventeenth century, the terms denization and naturalization were still often used interchangeably and the term denization can be found in Acts of Parliament.

Few records of individual denization and naturalization appear before 1509, the year in which Henry VIII came to the throne. It is important to note that the vast majority of those settling in the United Kingdom did not go through the legal formalities of denization or naturalization as these processes were expensive and only the rich could afford them.

See chapter 6 for denization and naturalization sources from 1800 onwards.

5.3.1 Name Indexes to Citizenship Records

The central means of reference to citizenship records are the indexes to denization and naturalization. These surname indexes, published or unpublished, can be found in the National Archives reading rooms located alongside the Home Office (HO) series lists, and consist of copies of the following works: W. Page, *Denization and Naturalization of Aliens in England, 1509–1603* (Huguenot Society, vol. VIII, Lymington, 1893) and W. A. Shaw, *Letters of Denizen and Acts of Naturalization for Aliens in England, 1603–1800* (Huguenot Society, Lymington, 1911, Manchester, 1923 and London, 1932).

These publications can be found among the Home Office (HO) series lists in the reading rooms on the open shelves and the publications include transcriptions of the naturalization records themselves including naturalizations by private Act of Parliament, the original records

FIG. 22 *Henry Hansforth's 1431 petition to parliament.* SC 8/25

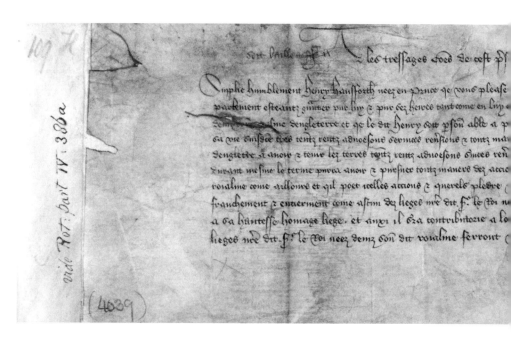

being housed in the Parliamentary Archives.

Although the indexes are *complete* in the sense that they claim to list all those persons who were successful in securing British nationality, not all the records to which they refer survive.

5.3.2   *Denization documentary sources*

In the case of denization applications, an applicant would first present a petition. The earliest examples of these petitions date from 1800. What survive from before this date are the signet bills – the impressed seal or stamp ordering the grant of denization to be drawn up. The key finding aid to these records are the Signet Office docquet books (SO 3), which contain short summaries of the signet bills kept by the clerks of the signet for the purpose of calculating the fees that were due. The docquet books contain both details of the bills that gave rise to instruments sealed within the signet, and of immediate warrants sent from the king to the Lord Chancellor, upon the latter of which the clerk levied fees. They are indexed, by name of applicant, in the series SO 4.

A duplicate series of docquet books created for the information of the Secretary of State for the period 1541–1761 can be found in SP 38, whilst the king's bills can be found in SP 39 for 1567–1645 and SP 7 for 1661–1851. A small number of original letters patent of denization are to be found in C 97, suggesting that the documents in this series were unclaimed by the patentees. With one exception from 1830, the original patents in series C 97 all date from the period 1752–92.

Letters of denizen were enrolled on Patent Rolls and are often

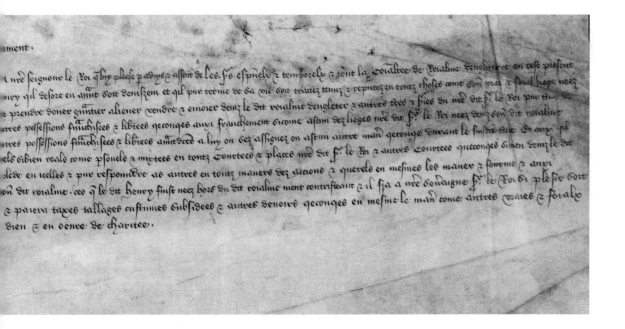

referred to as letters patent of denization. Letters of denizen are fully described and indexed in the printed calendars of Patent Rolls which are available in the Map and Large Document Room. The terms of the letters patent of denization varied at times in accordance with the provisions of the general Acts of Parliament passed to govern the status of aliens residing in England.

5.3.3 Naturalization documentary sources

Original private bills of naturalization presented to Parliament from 1497 are in the custody of the Parliamentary Archives: *www.parliament.uk/publications/archives.cfm*. Abstracts of the bills can be found in the published editions of *Journals of the House of Lords* and *Journals of the House of Commons*. Copies of these publications are held at The National Archive Library and other major reference libraries.

Lists of those taking oaths before the Quarter Sessions may survive locally at county record offices in Quarter Session records. Check Access to Archives at *www.nationalarchives.gov.uk/a2a* to see the availability and location of such records.

5.4 The Jewish Community

The Jewish community had a presence in England from the Norman Conquest, when Jews came over in the wake of William the Conqueror, until Edward I expelled them in 1290. In the early 1100s, Henry I granted the Jews a number of privileges: a Jew could, for example, acquit himself in a court of law if he found one Jew and one Christian to testify to his innocence, or, if he could find no witnesses, by swearing on a scroll of the Hebrew Pentateuch. Jurisdiction in cases involving Jews was reserved to royal courts or to the constables of royal castles in places where Jews lived. They became in effect royal chattels in return for royal protection. In 1201, King John confirmed the liberties granted to the Jews by Henry I (C 53/4, membrane 5). The Jews paid 4,000 marks for the privileges granted by the charter. No line of descent has been established from the members of this early community.

Jews were ordered to leave the country before the Feast of All Saints (1 November). Any who remained after that date were liable to the death penalty. They were allowed to take with them ready money and personal property and any unredeemed pledges of Christians, but bonds and real estate became the property of the Crown. Letters patent were directed to the bailiffs, barons and sailors of the Cinque Ports to provide safe conduct for Jews leaving the realm with their wives, children and goods (C 66/109, m. 14). The Archae were brought to London, together with other bonds and obligations, and inquisitions were held by the sheriffs into the houses and tenements of the Jews. Much of the property was given to royal favourites. A roll of grants of Jews' houses in various counties and the synagogues at Oxford, Norwich, Canterbury and Hereford survives in c 67/4, m. 2. A few Jews continued to enter England after the expulsion, but those who lived in the country for any length of time were converts to Christianity.

5.4.1 Expulsion and Resettlement

In 1656 the Lord Protector, Oliver Cromwell, permitted Jews to resettle in England. The Council of State granted passes of safe conduct to Manasseh ben Israel, scholar and rabbi of Amsterdam. He arrived in October 1655 and presented himself to the Council, but it was not

FIG. 23 *Manasseh ben Israel's petition of October 1655.* SP 18/101

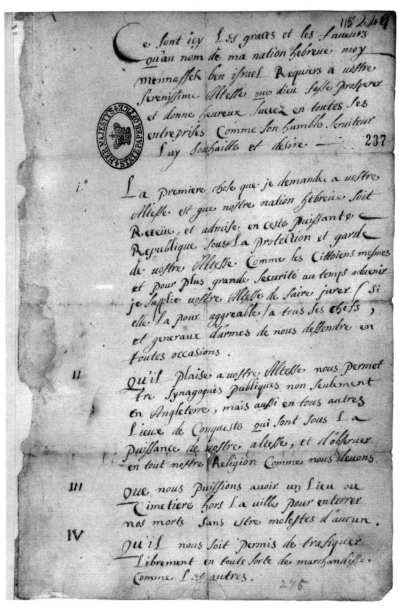

until 13 November that his petition and a humble address were referred to a committee of the council for consideration. The petition SP 18/101, F. 115 asked that the Jews might be permitted to live in England, have synagogues and cemeteries, and trade freely. Jewish disputes were to be settled by Mosaic law and all laws against the Jews would be repealed. It was quickly decided by the lawyers that there was no legal bar to re-admission. The committee made its report to the Council of State (SP 18/101, F. 118) setting out the objections made at the conference, but also reporting that there was no legal bar to the admission, though they laid down several conditions.

Spanish Marranos or Sephardic Jews had been forced to quit their country or convert, and their legal position was brought to a head following the outbreak of war with Spain when one of their number was arrested: Antonio Robles, a Marrano resident in London who was detained on suspicion of being an enemy alien. After a thorough investigation, the Council of State discharged Robles and ordered the return of his goods. While his case was being heard, Manasseh ben Israel and six leading Marranos resident in London petitioned the Lord Protector as Jews asking for permission in writing for Jews to meet for worship in their houses and to bury their dead outside the city (SP 18/125, F. 58). No reply or order of the Council of State appears to be extant, but the Jews must have received some assurance as they continued to live in London. In December 1656 they rented land in Creechurch Lane for a synagogue. Today, a plaque marks its site as the first synagogue established after resettlement.

The immigrants arriving from the 1650s were Sephardi (Portuguese, Spanish and Italian) and later, during the 1680s, Ashkenazi (central and eastern European) who arrived in the 1680s from Holland and Bohemia (the main influx of Ashkenazim from Russia and Poland was not until the end of the nineteenth century). By about 1690 there were enough German Jews for a separate Ashkenazi community in the city of London. Their first synagogue, the Great Synagogue, was opened in 1722.

5.5 The Black Community

The first black settlement in Britain began in the sixteenth century as a result of voyages to Africa and the development of the slave trade. From that point on, Africans became increasingly common in the ports of England. One of the earliest references, however, is not to a slave or to a seaman, but to a trumpeter in the household of Henry VII and Henry VIII. There is an entry in the accounts of the Treasurer of the Chamber dated 7 December 1507 of the payment of 20 shillings for 'John Blanke, the blacke trumpet, for his moneth wages of Novembre last passed at viii d the day' (E 36/214). He may even be the black trumpeter who appears on the illustrated Westminster Tournament Roll of 1511 (College of Arms Ms: MM. 4 and 28), held to celebrate the birth of a short-lived son to Catherine of Aragon. A facsimile reproduction of this is available in the National Archives Library and Resource Centre.

In 1596 Elizabeth I ordered that black people should be sent abroad and in 1601 a proclamation was issued stating that 'the great number of Negroes and Blackamoors which have crept into this realm' should be 'with all speed avoided and discharged out of this her majesty's dominions' (*Acts of the Privy Council*, xxvi, 1596–7, 16, 20 and 21). In practice, however, the number of Africans continued to grow in the seventeenth and eighteenth centuries.

There were two overlapping groups – the slaves and the free black community. The free community grew up in the ports of London, Liverpool and Bristol where there were communities of sailors and former slaves and their descendants. Planters and merchants brought back slaves from their plantations to become domestic servants. They might in time have gained their freedom, or they might have run away and lost themselves in London or the large ports. It is not always easy to trace people of colour among the records as one is normally dependent on them being designated as such. It is possible to find occasional references among the State Papers (SP), and parish registers (held locally) should always be consulted.

Wills of the aristocracy, gentry and merchant classes proved in the Prerogative Court of Canterbury (PROB), the Prerogative Court of York (held at the Borthwick Institute *www.york.ac.uk/inst/bihr*) and in the diocesan courts (diocesan/county record offices) can yield information on servants and former slaves. For example, in the will of Colonel Richard Bathurst of the Close, Lincoln in 1756, the free status of Francis Barber was confirmed when he was bequeathed his freedom and a legacy of £12 (PROB 11/824, SIG. 216).

Many middle-class households in the eighteenth century might have employed a black servant. Estate papers of families connected with the slave trade and the West Indies could also be researched. For this, use the National Register of Archives available online at *www.national archives.gov.uk/nra* and also Access to Archives (A2A) at *www. nationalarchives.gov.uk/a2a*.

5.5.1 *Committee for the Relief of the Black Poor, 1786*

Records of the Committee for the Relief of the Black Poor, 1786, are to be found in T1 Treasury Board Papers (T 1/631–6, 638, 641–7). These include minutes of the committee (T 1/631–8 and T 1/641) and Henry Smeathman's plan for the settlement of Sierra Leone (T 1/631/1304).

This scheme was proposed by the committee to solve the problem of poverty among the black community in London. On agreeing to leave the country and live in the new settlement in Sierra Leone the volunteers received a bounty payment. Of those who signed the contract to daughter of the said Thomas Clark one hundred Pounds for the trouble and hardships she has undergone thro' my not being able to pay her father what I owe him Also I give to Francis Barber a Negroe whom I brought from Jamaica aforesaid into England his freedom and twelve Pounds in Money Also I give unto the said Peter Lely fifty Pounds for the trouble he shall have in the Trust hereby in him reposed and I make the said Peter Lely Executor of this my last Will and Testament all the Rest of my Goods and Chattels and Personal Estate I give unto my Son Richard Bathurst In Witness whereof I have hereunto sett my hand and Seal this Twenty fourth day of Aprill in the Year of our Lord One thousand seven hundred and fifty four 1754 — Rich. Bathurst — Sealed Signed Published and declared to be his last Will and Testament of the Testator in the presence of us who subscribed our names as Witnesses and in the presence of the said Testator — Georg: Thompson Butcher in Lincoln — Job Dakin — Henry Flea Servants to Mrs Turner in Lincoln.

On the fourteenth day of August in the Year of our Lord One thousand seven hundred and fifty six. Administration with the Will annexed of all and singular the Goods Chattels and Credits of Richard Bathurst late of the Close of Lincoln in the County of Lincoln deceased was granted to Richard Bathurst the Son of the deceased and residuary Legatee named in the said Will he having been first sworn duly to administer ...

FIG. 24 *Colonel Richard Bathurst's will, giving Francis Barber his freedom.* PROB 11/824

go to Sierra Leone, not everyone actually went, and of those who did, many perished or became slaves or slave traders themselves when the settlement failed shortly after being established.

5.6 German Immigrants

There has been a significant German presence in London since the twelfth century. The merchants of the Hanseatic League were granted privileges in the city, and the Steelyard became the centre of an important community that elected its own aldermen. Other German merchants had connections with the ports of the east coast: Ipswich, Yarmouth, King's Lynn, Boston, Hull and Newcastle.

The National Archives holds a collection of registers from German Lutheran chapels in London. These can be found in RG 4, which is available online to search and download at *www.bmdregisters.co.uk*. Access to the database and images of non-conformist (non-parochial) registers of births, marriages and deaths in England and Wales between 1567 and 1840 is free in the reading rooms. It includes other foreign churches, such as those relating to Russian immigrants and Dutch immigrants. The London Metropolitan Archives has records of the German Hamburg Lutheran Church (LMA ref: ACC/2622) and of other German churches. The Anglo-German Family History Society has produced microfiche indexes to St George's German Lutheran Church records.

6 NATURALIZATION AND CITIZENSHIP AFTER 1800

The tradition by which aliens resident in Britain attempted to improve their lot through becoming naturalized or applying to the Crown for letters of denizen continued into the nineteenth century. The citizenship records generated are some of the richest sources for family historians. Depending on the date you can establish a host of facts, including where precisely he or she came from and each address they occupied over a period of five years. In addition, there may be detailed references to their spouse, children and parents, as well as to neighbours and friends who may have vouched for their respectability when they applied to become British. Memorial records, which are not available for those researching ancestors before 1800, are particularly valuable in this regard. However, the legal formalities of denization or naturalization remained prohibitively expensive and only the rich could afford them.

6.1 Sources for Citizenship Policy Records

Citizenship policy documents at The National Archives include general files relating to policy concerning denization (which decreased after 1844 and had likely discontinued by 1873), naturalization by private act of parliament, naturalization by certificate of Secretary of State, naturalization under acts of the Irish parliament, Channel Islands naturalization, and colonial and foreign naturalization. They also include personal files rich in genealogical material.

6.1.1 *Before 1940*
Before 1940 Departmental policy files relating to the subject of citizenship can be found in Home Office registered papers in HO 45 and HO 144. Descriptions of these pieces can be found on the Catalogue for these two series, which deal with a range of subjects, reflecting the diversity of matters dealt with by the Home Office. HO 162 consists of entry books of out-letters relating to various aspects (including policy matters) of the working of the Aliens Act 1905, the Aliens Restriction Act 1914 and subsequent legislation.

HO 213 contains general (GEN) policy files of the Aliens Department. The files deal with the definition of British and foreign nationality, along with a wide variety of related topics including naturalizations, immigration, refugees, internees and prisoners of war, the employment of foreign labour, deportation, and the status of citizens of the Irish Republic. There are also papers relating to departmental committees, statistics, conferences, conventions and treaties on these subjects. The GEN series began in the late 1930s as 'Aliens General'.

In 1949 the Home Office replaced the six-figure file series of general correspondence with separate series of files for each subject or function, each distinguished by letter symbols. Legislation relating to the control of immigration and nationality policy may be found in a number of series, such as:

HO 352 Aliens, General Matters (ALG Symbol Series) Files 1945–73
HO 367 Aliens Department and Immigration and Nationality
     Department: Organization (ALO and IMO Symbol Series) Files
     1961–2
HO 394 Immigration General (IMG Symbol Series) Files 1961–75

Some pieces within these series contain administrative histories of the departmental functions and responsibilities for immigration and citizenship policy and legislation. Examples include HO 352/51 The Alien Problem, memorandum by P. Conlan; HO 352/53 Aliens Control in the Nineteenth Century, memorandum by D.E. Faulkner; and HO 367/1 History of Immigration and Nationality Department (IND).

6.2 Name Indexes to Citizenship Records

A key means of reference to citizenship records are the unpublished indexes compiled by Home Office departmental staff to denizations 1801–73, and to acts of naturalization, 1801–1900, and indexes to naturalizations granted by the Secretary of State for Home Affairs, 1844–1980. Copies of yearly indexes up to 1961 can also be found among the series of Parliamentary papers available via OPERA (Online publications and electronic resources). Although the Parliamentary papers do not provide Home Office references or certificate numbers, they often list full addresses of applicants, which can be used in conjunction with the decennial census returns, 1841–1911.

While indexes covering the period before 1800 often provide full transcriptions of documents, those listing naturalizations and denizations after 1800 do not. However, in addition to names, the denization index for 1800–73 lists country of origin and details of rights conferred, while the index to naturalization by Secretary of State for 1844–1980 lists country of origin and place of residence. These indexes are a useful tool for social historians and local historians examining patterns of immigration in local communities in the nineteenth and twentieth centuries.

Although these indexes are *complete* in the sense that they claim to list *all* those persons who were successful in securing British nationality from 1509 to 1980, not all the records to which they refer survive. Remember that they only list those who acquired naturalization by Act of Parliament or by application to the Secretary of State (from 1844). They will not include details of women of alien nationality who became British through marriage to a British subject before 1948. Also, when using the lists, remember to check variants in spelling or anglicizing of surnames. Similarly, don't forget to look under both former and new name if the person you are researching changed it. Until the beginning of 1916 aliens resident in Britain could change their names like British subjects, but enemy aliens (Austrians, Germans and Turks) were then forbidden by Order in Council to do so. This rule was extended by the Aliens Restriction (Amendment) Act 1919 (as amended by reg. 20 of the Defence (General) Regulations 1939) to all aliens.

FIG. 25 *An original patent of denization from 1843.* HO 4/51

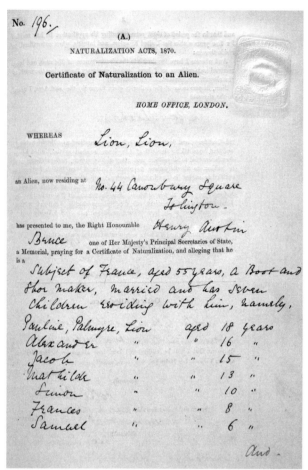

No. 196.

(A.)

NATURALIZATION ACTS, 1870.

Certificate of Naturalization to an Alien.

HOME OFFICE, LONDON.

WHEREAS *Lion, Lion,*

an Alien, now residing at *No. 44 Canonbury Square Islington.*

has presented to me, the Right Honourable *Henry Austin Bruce* one of Her Majesty's Principal Secretaries of State, a Memorial, praying for a Certificate of Naturalization, and alleging that he is a

Subject of France, aged 55 years, a Boot and Shoe maker, married and has seven Children residing with him, namely,

Pauline, Palmyre, Lion   aged 18 years
Alexander   "   "   16   "
Jacob   "   "   15   "
Mathilde   "   "   13   "
Simon   "   "   10   "
Frances   "   "   8   "
Samuel   "   "   6   "

And.

FIG. 26 *Duplicate Home Office naturalization certificate of 1875 for Lion Lion listing his seven children.*
HO 334/1

Exemption was possible only when a new name was assumed by Royal Licence or by special permission of the Home Secretary, or when a woman assumed her husband's surname on marriage. Exemptions in the first two series were advertised in the *London Gazette.* There are now no restrictions attached to a change of name effected in the United Kingdom by an overseas national. The parts of the Aliens Restriction (Amendment) Act relating to this were repealed by the Statute Law (Repeal) Act 1971. The Defence (General) Regulations lapsed some years previously.

Name indexes to naturalization do not include unsuccessful applicants.

The nominal lists for naturalizations granted in the period 1801–1935 have now been added to the Catalogue, allowing you to search by full name, nationality, place of residence and date of naturalization of applicant. This allows researchers to identify documents containing the background papers within the series HO 1 (1800–71), HO 45 (1872–8) and HO 144 (1879–1935).

You can already search by name and date of birth for background papers for the period 1935 to 1948 in the series HO 405. However, these records are still being transferred from the Home Office (see 2.3.1 for more details).

6.3   Grants Overseas

Files on individuals who were granted certificates of naturalization by governments of British possessions overseas may be found in CO 323, CO 1032 and DO 35 and also relevant CO and DO country correspondence series. Duplicate Overseas or 'O' certificates commencing in 1915 may be found in HO 334.

Additional information regarding certificates of naturalization and certificates of British nationality granted by governments of British possessions overseas, such as original applications of naturalization, may be found in the original correspondence series for the colony or dominion in which the certificate was granted, by referring to the relevant CO, DO and FCO series. In some cases, duplicate copies of certificates of British nationality granted by colonial governments are housed with British High Commissions. The FCO website can provide relevant contact details at *www.fco.gov.uk/travel*.

Certificates can also be found in the archives of the relevant country. For example, prior to 26 January 1949, the process of naturalization automatically conferred British nationality on applicants in the Commonwealth of Australia. It was not until the British Nationality Act 1948 that the concept of a separate Australian nationality was born. The National Archives of Australia have pre-federation British naturalization records from 1852 which normally consist of a Memorial for Letters of Naturalization (the application), Oath of Memorialist (i.e. the applicant) and Certificate and Oath of Allegiance. Records after 1904 may also include a Statutory Declaration, Application for Certificate of Naturalization and some routine correspondence. Applicants for many of these can be searched by name on the RecordSearch database on the *www.naa.gov.au* website.

6.4 Individual Denization and Naturalization Records

There are three main forms of record relating to citizenship. Firstly, from 1801, there are memorial documents presented by the applicant wishing to gain British nationality. Secondly, there are government departmental records concerning the application of the individual and background papers pertaining to the individual (where they survive, departmental papers are filed with the individual memorials). Finally, there are duplicate copies of certificates of nationality presented to successful applicants, and other official records such as copies of naturalization, Acts of Parliament and denizen letters patent.

6.5 Tracing Memorial Records

No memorial papers survive before 1800. From 1801, memorial documents and background departmental records are filed together to form one record. Memorial records consist of a petition by the applicant and, in many instances, an affidavit supporting the application. Departmental records may include investigations carried out by local authorities concerning the suitability of the candidate.

Before any general naturalization legislation was introduced in 1844, and before the Home Office became actively involved in the granting of naturalizations, there were no general requirements to govern the content of the memorial. Following the Naturalization Act (7 and 8 Vict. c. 66), every alien who had the intention of becoming a British citizen was required to present a memorial to the Secretary of

State stating age, trade and duration of residence. Thereupon the Secretary of State would issue to the applicant a certificate granting rights of a natural-born subject with the exception of the right of being of the Privy Council or Parliament. The Act maintained the taking of the oath of allegiance and Act of Succession and provided that any woman married to a natural-born or naturalized person was deemed naturalized herself. It further stipulated that applicants wishing to become naturalized citizens should state their intention to reside and settle in Great Britain.

After the 1847 Act was passed, a declaration signed by at least four householders was required. Each householder, known as a resident referee, had to state their place of residence, vouch for the respectability and loyalty of the applicant, and verify the several particulars stated in the memorial. These declarations were to be made before a magistrate and the referees themselves were accepted only if they met the following criteria: they were natural-born British subjects, were not the agents or solicitors of the applicant, were able to testify to the facts of residence from personal knowledge, and had known the applicant for at least five years.

The 1870 Naturalization Act (33 and 34 Vict. c. 14) was even more demanding. Applicants now had to have been resident within the United Kingdom for at least five years before submitting an application, in addition to declaring their intention to reside permanently in the country. After 1870, memorialist records include name and address of applicant, names and addresses of any children residing with him or her and the addresses of any residences occupied by him or her during the five-year qualification period. From 1880 an additional resident referee was required specifically to verify the times and addresses and periods of residence during the five-year qualification period.

The practice of obtaining a Metropolitan Police report on the respectability of the applicant and referees was established in 1873. This was in part due to the activities of certain Belgians and Germans who had committed offences in their respective countries and attempted to apply for naturalization so as to avoid extradition from the United Kingdom. Outside London, mayors and chairmen of Quarter Sessions were asked to inquire into candidates' respectability and referees.

Once the 1914 Act was passed, applicants were expected to have an adequate knowledge of English, and memorials after this Act include supervised English proficiency tests.

6.5.1   *Denizations, 1801–73*
For Home Office papers and memorial papers resulting from denizations, search by name on the Catalogue. There are three sources of Home Office background papers and memorial papers for this period:

HO 1/6–12 for patents issued 1801–40

FIG. 27 *John George
Dill's Petition of
denization from
1817.* HO 1/7

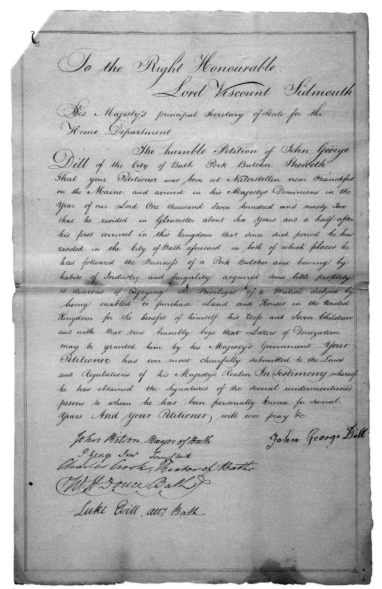

HO 44/44–9 for patents issued 1801–32 (within the HO 44 series
list there is a separate index to persons, corporate bodies and
places which provides folio references within documents)

HO 45 for patents issued 1841–73. (The piece number for this
series is simply converted from the 'OS' – Old Series – number
listed in the 'HO number' column.)

6.5.2 *Naturalization by Act of Parliament, 1802–1900*

Search by name on the Catalogue. There are three sources of memorial
papers for this period:

HO 1/13–16 for correspondence 1802–58
HO 45 for correspondence 1841–78
HO 144 for correspondence 1879–1900.

6.5.3 *Naturalization granted by the Home Office, 1844–1922*

Search by name on the Catalogue. There are three sources of memorial papers for this period:

HO 1/17–176 for correspondence 1800–71
HO 45 for correspondence 1872–8
HO 144 for correspondence 1879–1922.

6.5.4 *Tracing memorial records after 1922*

Memorial papers for naturalizations after 1922 are closed to public inspection. However, you can request a review of the information contained in the files of persons naturalized between 1922 and 1948 under the Freedom of Information Act 2000. You can do this by following the prompts on the Catalogue at piece level in HO 144 or HO 405. The Home Office is opening an increasing number of records dated after 1922, but some records will remain closed to maintain confidentiality. Since the basis for closure is usually the personal sensitivity of the information – and this is generally only regarded as sensitive for the lifetime of the individual – researchers who can provide evidence that the individual is dead will be assisting the Home Office considerably in determining whether the file can be opened, although there may, of course, be continuing sensitivities in regard to other people mentioned in the file.

HO 405 includes post-1934 applications for naturalization made by people who arrived in the UK before 1948, where the file has survived. This represents an estimated 40 per cent of all such cases, so the collection constitutes a very large sample, preserved exceptionally to show the handling of refugees in a period of political turmoil (other files were destroyed under Statute). To date, those for surnames A–N are included on the Catalogue. See 2.3.1 for more details.

6.5.5 *Tracing unsuccessful applications*

The vast majority of files relating to unsuccessful applications for naturalization have not been preserved as archives. Where they survive they can be found, together with departmental papers, in HO 45 for the period between 1844 and 1879 and HO 144 thereafter. There is no complete index to these records and references to any surviving records may be found in the list relating to the subject heading 'Naturalization', in the main lists for both these series rather than in the separate indexes to naturalizations.

HO 5 includes out-letters and entry books of the Home Office and the Aliens Office relating to aliens and registers of applications for denization. The series covers the period 1794–1921, though for 1871–3, such out-letters will be found in HO 136. These records include registers of applications for naturalization for the period 1798–1829 (HO 5/34–7), which record name of applicant, date of arrival in the United Kingdom, place of residence and date of certificate if granted. The series covers the period 1794–1921, though for the period 1871–3 such out-letters will be found in HO 136. HO 5 is being digitized and the records should be searchable by name and the results downloaded at *www.ancestry.co.uk* from spring 2009.

Previous unsuccessful applications are preserved alongside successful ones in HO 405. As stated above, this series is in the process of being transferred to the National Archives. See 2.3.1 for more details.

FIG. 28 *A memorial paper from 1864. Naturalization was refused due to 'doubtful character'.* HO 45/7525

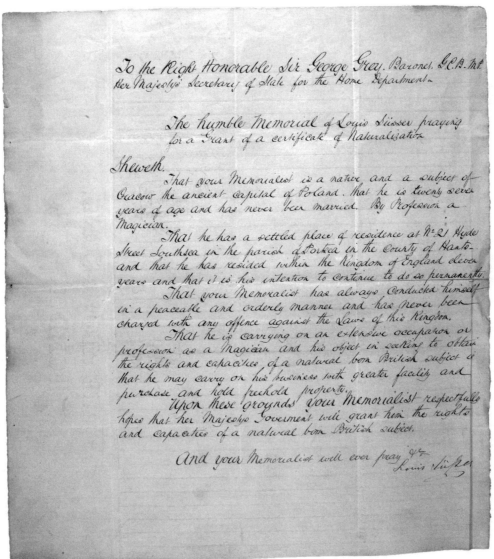

6.6 Tracing Acts of Parliament and Letters Patent

These documents are official government records recording the fact that citizenship rights were granted to individuals. Later records were required as legal evidence to prove that naturalization was granted and where any other official copy had been lost. Individuals often needed to present proof that citizenship rights had been conferred in order to obtain other documents and entitlements such as passports, marriage certificates and to prove pension rights. Information provided in these documents is usually restricted to full name, country of origin and the date when citizenship rights were conferred and – for the period before 1800 – such information has been included in the nominal indexes (see 6.2).

6.6.1 *Denizations by letters patent, 1800–1873*

In order to trace an entry for letters patent for denizations after 1800 you will need to refer to a series of finding aids to Patent Rolls and other Chancery Rolls known as Palmer's Indexes, in IND 1/17276–428. The indexes are arranged chronologically. The indexes refer to entries of denization by letters patent entered on the Patent Rolls and supplementary Patent Rolls in C 66 and C 67 between 1801 and 1844, when responsibility passed to the Home Office. Draft letters patent for denizations between 1830 and 1873 can be found in C 197/29. Original patents of denization can be found in HO 4 (see Fig. 25).

A roll of warrants for letters of denizen for the City of Westminster is held at the Westminster Abbey Muniments and Library.

6.6.2 *Naturalizations by Act of Parliament*

For acts after 1800, consult *Index to Local and Personal Acts* (1949), a copy of which is held in the National Archives Library. Once again, copies of the acts may be found in the Parliamentary Archives. Abstracts of these private acts of naturalization are contained in the published editions of *Journals of the House of Lords* and *Journals of the House of Commons*. Copies of these publications are held in the National Archives Library.

6.7 Tracing Citizenship Certificate Records, 1844–1987

Certificate documents consist of departmental copies of the certificates of naturalization or British nationality issued to successful applicants. Essentially, the certificate document contains a summary of information supplied in the memorial itself, namely: name of applicant, address, trade or occupation, place and date of birth, nationality, marital status, name of spouse (if applicable) and names and nationalities of parents. Between 1844 and 1873 certificates of naturalization were copied onto parchment and the copies then enrolled on the Close Rolls.

After 1870 they were bound together in volumes (usually of 500 certificates) in the Home Office. Duplicate copies of certificates of British nationality after the British Nationality Act 1948 are also filed in this way.

Certificates issued after 1 October 1986 are available via the UK Border Agency, though restrictions apply to those issued less than 10 years ago.

6.7.1 *Naturalization certificates, 1844–70*

Certificates of naturalization granted by the Secretary of State were enrolled on the Court of Chancery Close Rolls (C 54) from August 1844 to August 1873. In order to trace entries for certificates of naturalization for these dates you will first need to find the date of certificate provided on the Catalogue and then refer to the series of finding aids to Close Rolls and other Chancery Rolls known as Palmer's Indexes, in IND 1/17276–428. The indexes are arranged chronologically.

6.7.2 *Naturalization certificates, 1870–1987*

For the period 1870–1935, you can search by full name, nationality, place of residence, and date of naturalization on the Catalogue. Resulting searches provide the number of the certificate usually prefixed by a letter or series of letters (e.g. AZ), depending on the legislation in force governing the issuing of certificates. Using the certificate number, you can trace the certificate itself in the series HO 334 – there are sub-sections for each type of certificate issued (Fig. 26). Certificates in this series are filed together in numerical order and chronologically, usually in volumes of 500 certificates. It is therefore important to remember the certificate number so you can find the right certificate when the document arrives.

If you cannot find a reference in the online Catalogue for your case, or your case happened after 1935, then consult the name indexes to naturalizations, which can be found among the series of Additional Finding Aids in the Open Reading Room for the period 1937–80 (annual name indexes up to 1961 are available in Parliamentary papers online in the Open Reading Room on OPERA – the National Archives online published electronic resources). Please note that indexes for certificates issued after 1 October 1986 are held by the Home Office UK Border Agency in Liverpool (*nationality enquiries@ukba.gsi.gov.uk*).

HO 334 contains duplicates of certificates and declarations granted by the Home Secretary under the Naturalization Act 1870, the British Nationality and Status of Aliens Act 1914 and the British Nationality Act 1948. The various types of certificates granted under these Acts are listed here:

Naturalization Act 1870: certificates of naturalization

Certificate A	certificate (ordinary) to a person with five years' residence in the United Kingdom during the eight years immediately preceding application for naturalization.
Certificate AA	certificate to a person with five years' service under the Crown during the eight years immediately preceding application for naturalization.
Certificate AAA	certificate to a person in the Diplomatic or Consular Service with five years' service under the Crown during the eight years immediately preceding application for naturalization.
Certificate B	certificate to a person who has already been granted a certificate of naturalization under the act of 1844.
Certificate C	certificate to a person of 'doubtful nationality', with five years' residence in the United Kingdom, or five years' service under the Crown, during the eight

FIG. 29 *Special certificate of naturalization (certificate 'C') for the Bavarian-born artist Hubert von Herkomer.* HO 334/1

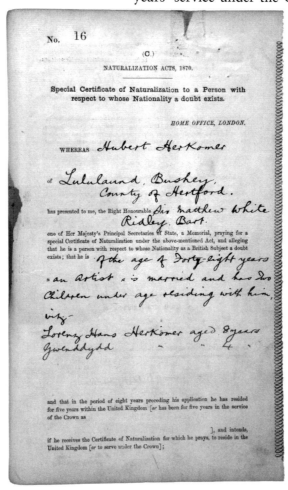

	years immediately preceding application for re-admission.
Certificate D	certificate of re-admission of person to British nationality with five years' residence in the United Kingdom, or five years' service under the Crown, during the last eight years immediately preceding application for re-admission.
Certificate DA	certificate granted by the Governor of any British possession and registered in the Home Office, or re-admission of person with five years' residence in that possession, or with five years' service under the Crown, during the eight years immediately preceding application for re-admission.

Naturalization Act 1870: declarations of alienage

Declaration E	declaration by a person, a subject of a foreign state subsequently naturalized as a British subject, renouncing British nationality.
Declaration F	declaration by a person, an alien by origin but born within HM dominions, renouncing British nationality.
Declaration G	declaration by a person, born out of HM dominions to a father being a British subject, renouncing British nationality.

Naturalization Act 1870: declarations of British nationality

Declaration H	declaration by a natural-born British subject, renouncing subsequent naturalization in a foreign state.

British Nationality and Status of Aliens Act 1914: certificates of naturalization

Certificate A and AZ	certificate (ordinary) granted under Section 2 of the Act, where the names of children are not included.
Certificate B and BZ	similar to Certificate A, but including the names of children.
Certificate C and CZ	certificate granted under sub-section (2) of Section 5 of the Act to a minor.
Certificate D	special certificate granted under Section 4 of the Act to a person with respect to whose nationality a doubt exists, where the names of children are not included.
Certificate DZ	certificate of naturalization granted to a woman who was at birth a British subject and is married to a subject of a state at war with His Majesty.
Certificate E	similar to Certificate D, but including the names of children.

Certificate EZ	similar to Certificate DZ, but including the names of children.
Certificate F	certificate granted under Section 6 of the Act to a person naturalized before the passing of the Act, where the names of children are not included.
Certificate G	similar to Certificate F, but including the names of children.
Certificate GZ	similar to Certificate FZ, but including the names of children.
Certificate H	certificate granted under Section 10 of the Act to a woman who was at birth a British subject, and is married to a subject of a state at war with His Majesty, where the names of the children are not included.
Certificate I	similar to Certificate H, but including the names of children.
Certificate M	special certificate granted under Section 4 of the Act to a person with respect to whose nationality a doubt exists.
Certificate O	certificate granted under Section 8 of the Act by the government of a British possession overseas.

6.7.3   *Registration of British citizenship documents, 1948–87*

These documents are generally known as 'R' certificates and refer to registrations of British citizenship declared by a British subject or citizen of the Republic of Ireland or of the Channel Islands, Isle of Man, a colony, a protectorate or a protected state, or a UK Trust Territory under the British Nationality Act 1948. The National Archives hold Home Office copies and these may be found in the series HO 334. The certificates enabled colonial workers and families to migrate to Britain and settle with ease. Various certificates were issued under the Act:

Certificate BNA	application made by a subject of a foreign state resident in the UK.
Certificate M	(s7 and 18 1948 Act) application for registration of a minor child.
Certificate O	application made by a subject of a foreign state resident overseas.
Certificate R1	(s6(1) 1948 Act) application made by an adult British subject or citizen of the Republic of Ireland, or any of the Channel Islands, Isle of Man, a colony, a protectorate or a protected state to which s8(1) of the Act applied, or a UK Trust Territory, or on the grounds of Crown Service under HM Government in the UK.

Certificate R2	(s6 (2) 1948 Act) application made by a woman who has been married to a citizen of the UK and colonies.
Certificate R3	(s6 (2) 1948 Act) application made by a woman who has been married to a citizen of the UK and colonies.
Certificate R4	(s12 (6) 1948 Act) application made by a person who but for his citizenship or potential citizenship of one of the countries mentioned in s1 (3) of the Act would have become a citizen of the UK and colonies under s12 (4) of the Act.
Certificate R5	(s16 1948 Act) application to resume British nationality by a person who has ceased to be a British subject on the loss of British nationality by his father or mother in accordance with s12 (1) of the 1914 Act.
Certificate R6	(s19 1948 Act) declaration of citizenship made by a citizen of the UK and colonies who is also a citizen of one of the countries mentioned in s13 of the Act or of the Republic of Ireland or is a national of a foreign country.

'R' certificates were issued under the British Nationality Act 1948, which came into effect on 1 January 1949, and duplicate Home Office copies may be found in the series HO 334. The actual original registration of nationality forms part of the certificate. Usually, the certificates provide the applicant's (and spouse's) name, address and date and place of birth, the applicant's father's name, and the nationality of the applicant.

The National Archives has recently acquired name indexes to the registration of British citizenship certificates. These are arranged alphabetically and give name, date of birth, certificate number and date when the certificate was granted. There is no public access to these indexes, although the National Archives will check them on behalf of enquirers. If you need to trace an 'R' certificate for which the certificate number is unknown, you will need to provide the following information:

Full name of applicant
Date of birth
Place of registration
Date of registration.

The certificates at the National Archives are arranged by certificate number, so, unless this is known, researchers may need to contact the Department in writing prior to visiting the National Archives.

The National Archives only holds duplicate registrations of British nationality for those registrations made in the UK and processed by the Home Office, London. Those registered (still prefixed by the various R categories R1–R6) in British possessions and colonies would have been processed by the government of the relevant colony. In such cases, the appropriate British High Commission should be contacted to see if a copy of the registration survives there. Contact details of British High Commissioners can be found on the internet at *www.fco.gov.uk/travel*.

It should be noted that from June 1969 until 1987 the Home Office did not maintain a set of duplicate naturalization certificates (these were successors to the BNA certificates). Anyone requiring confirmation of naturalization for this period (often a six-figure reference starting with 'o') should write to the UK Border Agency who will provide a letter of confirmation suitable for legal purposes. This will not, however, add to the information contained in the printed indexes available in the Open Reading Room.

6.8   Other Citizenship Records

Many aliens needed to submit declarations of alienage to the Home Office. Before a declaration could be registered, a certificate from some official authority, such as a consul, needed to be obtained to prove that the declaration was genuine. Surviving declarations of alienage registrations and correspondence can be found in HO 45.

Also included in these series is correspondence relating to certificates of British origin and special certificates of British origin, issued to coloured seamen, following the Special Restriction (Coloured Alien Seamen) Order, 1925.

6.9   Case Study

6.9.1   *Charles Soveral*
Charles Soveral was born in Paris, France on 18 May 1894 to Portuguese parents Edward Pinto and Ida Anna Alexandra Soveral. He was brought to England when 'not a month old'. It is not clear what happened to his father, but his mother married John Alexander Apcar, a British-born subject, soon after.

Charles' nationality remained Portuguese and in May 1917 he joined the British Army. Under the British Nationality and Status of Aliens Act 1914, friendly aliens serving in the British Army could apply for naturalization without having to pay the normal fee. Supporting his application was Lt-Colonel John Sheldon Hepworth, JP and solicitor in the firm of Hepworth and Co., Finsbury.

He had known Charles since he was 11 years old through his stepfather John Alexander Apcar, a barrister who had been called to the Bar at the Inner Temple on 17 November 1874. He gave Charles a glowing reference, describing him as of 'good moral character and having a complete knowledge of the English language, having been

Russia—D.

APPLICATION TO THE SECRETARY OF STATE BY A FRIENDLY ALIEN SERVING, OR ABOUT TO SERVE, IN THE BRITISH ARMY, FOR THE GRANT OF A CERTIFICATE OF NATURALIZATION, WITHOUT FEE, UNDER THE BRITISH NATIONALITY AND STATUS OF ALIENS ACT, 1914.

367947

(1) Full name *Charles Soveral. known as Charles Apcar for Last 19 years*

(If commonly known by a name other than his original name, state both)

(2) Whether registered under the Aliens Restriction Order *Yes*

If so, where *Cannon Row Metropolitan Police London*   Date of Registration *18 December 1916*

Serial No. *A Z 236.*

(3) Nationality *Portuguese*   Birthplace *Paris 23 Rue de la Faisanderie*

(*It is not sufficient to describe nationality as Polish or Jewish: the description should be e.g., Russian. The birthplace should be in the form of a postal address, showing the town, province and country.*)

(4) Age *24 last May*   Date of Birth *18 May 1894.*

(5) Present home address, or last address before enlistment *c/o Mrs John A Apcar, Baileys Hotel (Gloucester) Road. S.W.7., last address before enlistment was Hotel Windsor Victoria Street S.W.*

(6) How many years resident in this country? *24 years + 2½ months.*

(If residence broken by absence abroad for more than six months in any one of the last eight years, state the periods and places of absence.)

I was brought to England when not quite eight & have continuously resided in England since then

(7) Details of residence in the United Kingdom for the last 12 months. *I joined the British Army on 14 May 1917 which more than 12 months to date*

From	to	Address.	Months.	
2 Sept 1917	26 Oct 1917	Active Service B.E.F. France.	1	24
26 Oct 1917	2 April 1918	Military Hospitals London & Shirley near Croydon	5	7
2 April 1918	22 May 1918	Aisne Barracks Blackdown Camp	.1.	20
22 May 1918	30 August 1918	London Command Dept. Shoreham by Sea	3.	8
from 30 August 1918 on seven days leave Baileys Hotel Gloucester Road S.W.7			12 months.	2

(8) Details of residence in the United Kingdom or elsewhere in H.M. Dominions, covering four years in all, preceding and not including the last 12 months.

(*The dates and addresses should be clearly stated.*)

From	to	Address.	Years.	Months.	Days
2 Sept 1913	19 Nov 1913	329 Bath Road Hounslow	.	1.	17
19 Nov 1913	14 May 1917	Hotel Windsor Victoria Street S.W.1	3.	6.	25
14 May 1917	4 Aug. 1917	Aisne Barracks Blackdown Camp	.	2.	20
4 Aug 1917	2 Sept 1917	Active Service B.E.F. France	.	.	29
From	to	at	3.	9.	9
			= 4 years		

(s 7407) Wt. 21766—g427 15M 8/16 H & S

educated at Charterhouse, one of our well known public schools'.

Charles' occupation was a chartered accountant's clerk for Messrs Ball, Baker and Cornish and Co. at 1, Gresham Buildings, Basinghall Street in the City of London. He had been employed there since 1913, but on 14 May 1917, he joined the British Army as a private serving in the 1/5 City of London Regiment (London Rifle Brigade), regimental number 305621, in France between 14 May 1917 and 4 August 1917, returning about 26 October 1917. He was then a patient in the Military Hospitals London and Shirley, where he was reported to be in a delicate state of health and likely to remain permanently at Aisne Barracks, Blackdown Camp, near Farnborough, Aldershot. Prior to joining the army he had resided at 397 Bath Road, Hounslow, and Hotel Windsor, Victoria Street.

He applied for naturalization on 2 September 1918. The application was supported, verified and checked by the Criminal Investigation Department of the Metropolitan Police, who confirmed that nothing was recorded to the detriment of the memorialist. The application was successful and the certificate was made out on 15 November 1918 and dated 22 November 1918. Charles never had sight of the certificate as he was killed in action just three days before the war ended on 8 November 1918 and is buried in the Outrijve Churchyard.

Relevant records include:

HO 144/1501/367947 Nationality and Naturalization Memorial Papers: Soveral, Charles (known as Charles Apcar), from Portugal. Resident in London. Certificate 3940 made out 15 November 1918. Applicant killed in action 8 November 1918.

WO 95/2962 War Diary, 169 Infantry Brigade, 1/5 Battalion London Regiment (London Rifle Brigade), 1917–19.

7 BEYOND THE SEAS

Sources relating to involuntary migrants (mainly convicts sentenced to transportation) are discussed in chapter 8. Common sources relating to migration to general destinations, such as passenger lists, are discussed in chapter 1. This chapter looks specifically at emigration to the colonies and records relating to migration schemes and voluntary settlement there.

Britain, in common with other European countries, has always had a mobile population, but with the discovery of the Americas, and the development of trade routes to sub-Saharan Africa and the Orient, whole new vistas were opened up. Migration to the New World was driven by the opportunities it offered both individuals and authorities: to seek wealth, to start anew, to expand boundaries and to get rid of undesirables. The early colonists were merchants, pirates, buccaneers and adventurers. In their wake came large-scale migration that developed the land and built the economy.

Colonial populations were not static, however. After the American War of Independence, Loyalists left for Canada, Nova Scotia, the Bahamas and England. Also, after the abolition of slavery, emigrants from the Indian sub-continent were encouraged to migrate to the West Indies to help with local labour problems, as indentured/bonded labour.

In terms of scale, it is clear that emigration to the colonies was widespread from the seventeenth century onwards. It is estimated that around 1.7 million people left the UK during the seventeenth and eighteenth centuries. A further 10 million were to follow during the nineteenth and twentieth centuries.

7.1 General Sources

Although there are very many references in documents in the National Archives to individuals and families who left for the various colonies, there is sadly no single index to their names. There are, however, a number of general sources that can be consulted depending on destination.

7.1.1 Printed sources

Much of the information relating to emigration to the colonies has been printed in some form. Most of it is administrative in character, but it can include useful genealogical material. Main published sources include the records of the Privy Council (PC 1, 2 and 5), printed as *Acts of the Privy Council of England, Colonial Series*. Various useful early series of Treasury papers, registers and indexes, including T 1, 2, 3 and 4, and T 108, contain considerable reference to Colonial Office business. Many of these have been described and indexed in the published *Calendar of Treasury Papers, 1557–1728, Calendar of Treasury Books, 1660–1718*, and the *Calendar of Treasury Books and Papers, 1729–1745* and include reference to additional useful Treasury series.

Among these are T 7 Treasury: Books of Out-letters concerning Colonial Affairs 1849–1921, T 27 General Out-letter Books 1668–1920, T 28 Treasury: Various Out-letter Books 1763–1885, T 29 Minute Books 1667–1870, T 38 Treasury: Departmental Accounts 1558–1937, T 99 Minute Books, Supplementary 1690–1832, T 52 Entry Books of Royal Warrants 1667–1857, T 53 Entry Books of Royal Warrants Relating to the Payment of Money 1676–1839, T 54 Entry Books of Warrants concerning Appointments, Crown Leases and other 1667 to 1849, and T 60 Order Books, 1667–1831.

For senior civil servants posted overseas, see the British Imperial Calendar, which runs from 1810 to 1972, when it became the Civil Service Year Book. From 1852 there is the Foreign Office List, and from 1862 the Colonial Office List. The Diplomatic Service List runs from 1966, and the Commonwealth Relations Office List from 1953. All are on open access in the Open Reading Room at the National Archives. There is also, available in the Library area, the useful source David P. Henige, *Colonial Governors from the fifteenth century to the present: a comprehensive list* (1970).

7.1.2 Colonial Office and Foreign Office records

The records of the Colonial Office include much material relating to emigrants to all colonies. The series CO 384 *Emigration Original Correspondence 1817–1896* contains many personal letters from settlers or people intending to settle in the colonies. Those for British North America are in a separate register. Details of land grants and applications are in CO 323 *Colonies, General: Original Correspondence 1689–1952*, CO 324 *Colonies, General: Entry Books Series I 1662–1872* and CO 381 *Colonies, General: Entry Books Series II 1835–72*.

The Land and Emigration Commission was established in 1833 to promote emigration by providing free passage and land grants. The Emigration Entry Books, 1814–71 (CO 385) and the Land and Emigration Commission Papers, 1833–94 (CO 386) give names of emigrants, though there is no name index to these on the Catalogue. The series CO 386 also contains records of the South Australian Colonization

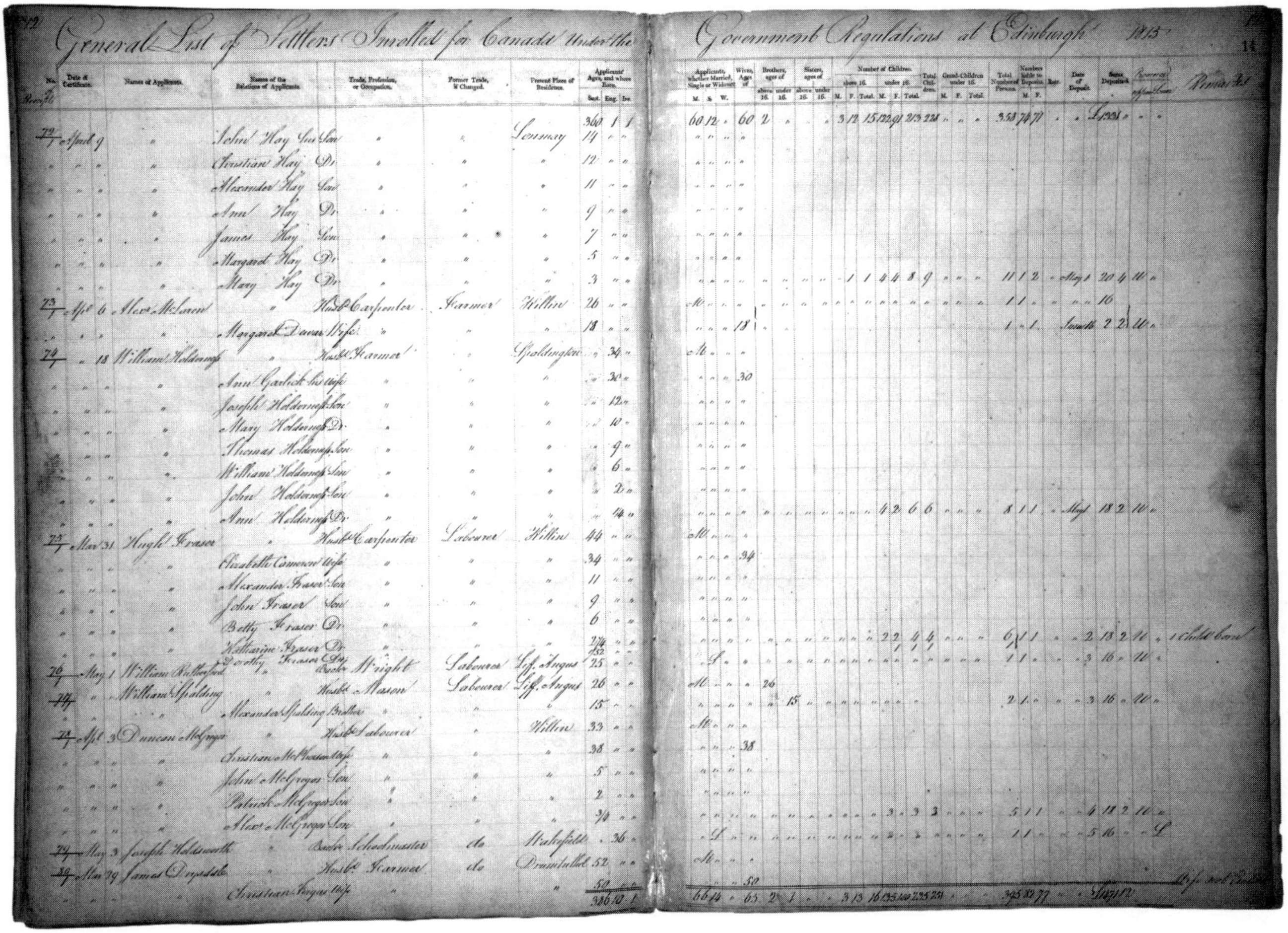

General List of Settlers Inrolled for Canada under the Government Regulations at Edinburgh 1815

No.	Date of Certificate	Names of Applicants	Names of the Relations of Applicants	Trade, Profession, or Occupation	Former Trade, if Changed	Present Place of Residence	Age
72	April 9	"	John Hay Jun. Son	"	"	Lenmay	14
"	"	"	Christian Hay Dr	"	"	"	12
"	"	"	Alexander Hay Son	"	"	"	11
"	"	"	Ann Hay Dr	"	"	"	9
"	"	"	James Hay Son	"	"	"	7
"	"	"	Margaret Hay Dr	"	"	"	5
"	"	"	Mary Hay Dr	"	"	"	3
73	Apl 6	Alexr McLaren	"	Husbd Carpenter	Farmer	Killin	26
"	"	"	Margaret Dewar Wife	"	"	"	18
74	" 18	William Holderness	"	Husbd Farmer	"	Spaldington	34
			Ann Garlick his Wife		"	"	30
			Joseph Holderness Son	"	"	"	12
			Mary Holderness Dr	"	"	"	10
			Thomas Holderness Son	"	"	"	9
			William Holderness Son	"	"	"	6
			John Holderness Son	"	"	"	2
			Ann Holderness Dr	"	"	"	1/4
75	Mar 31	Hugh Fraser	"	Husbd Carpenter	Labourer	Killin	44
			Elizabeth Cameron Wife	"	"	"	34
			Alexander Fraser Son	"	"	"	11
			John Fraser Son	"	"	"	9
			Betty Fraser Dr	"	"	"	6
			Katharine Fraser Dr				2/4
			Dorothy Fraser Dr				1/52
76	May 1	William Rutherford		Batchr Wright	Labourer	Lifft Angus	25
77	"	William Spalding		Husbd Mason	Labourer	Lifft Angus	26
			Alexander Spalding Brother		"		15
78	Apl 3	Duncan McGregor	"	Husbd Labourer	"	Killin	33
			Christian McPherson Wife		"	"	38
			John McGregor Son		"	"	5
			Patrick McGregor Son		"	"	2
			Alexr McGregor Son		"	"	1/4
79	May 3	Joseph Holdsworth	"	Batchr Schoolmaster	do	Wakefield	36
80	Mar 29	James Drysdale		Husbd Farmer	do	Drumtullel	52
			Christian [illegible] Wife			"	50

Fig. 31 *Details of emigrants to Canada in 1815.* CO 385/2

Commission, a predecessor of the Land and Emigration Commission, which was responsible for laying down the regulations for land sales and overseeing the selection of emigrants eligible for a free passage.

Entry books are among the most useful other colonial sources. These include details of patents and grants of land. Colonial government gazettes and colonial newspapers are similar in style and in the type of information they provide. As well as statistical information on subjects such as population, geography and accounts, they contain a wealth of information of specific interest to genealogists:

- Birth, marriage and death notifications (and occasionally obituaries)
- Notices of proceedings and sales in the local courts of Chancery and Petty Sessions
- Lists of people applying for liquor licences, dog licences, gun licences, etc.
- Lists of jurors, constables, nurses, druggists, solicitors, etc.
- Notices of sales of land, public appointments, leave of absence

and resumption of duty
Notices relating to cases of intestacy, wills, executors, etc.
Notices on applications for naturalization Inquests into wrecks
Lists of ships entering and clearing port, often with the names of
    first–class passengers
Lists of people in arrears of militia tax
Lists of people who paid parish relief.

They can also help to piece together the careers of colonial civil servants, recording appointments and promotions. References to individual colony series of government gazettes and colonial newspapers can
be found in the CO Index, available at the Research Enquiries Desk,
and also in A. Thurston, *Records of the Colonial Office, Dominions
Office, Commonwealth Relations Office and Commonwealth Office*
(1995). The British Library's Newspaper Library also holds an excellent collection of colonial newspapers and early gazettes:

Newspaper Library
The British Library
Colindale Avenue
London
NW9 5HE

Tel: 020 7412 7353
Email: *www.bl.uk/reshelp/inrrooms/blnewspapers/newsrr.html*
Website: *www.bl.uk*

The indexes to general correspondence of the Foreign Office can also
contain useful information. This may include reference to correspondence with overseas embassies and consulates. The general correspondence consists of the original papers accumulated in London, that is, the
original dispatches from British representatives abroad with any enclo-
sures: drafts of outgoing dispatches; minutes; domestic correspondence
with foreign representatives in this country, with other branches of the
British government and with private individuals and bodies.

Records earlier in date than 1906 are to be found in the series
FO 1–84, FO 90–2, and FO 95–111. For the most part, they are
arranged by country. In addition, there are some series of a general or
miscellaneous nature not related to a particular country. Departmental
diaries and registers, and general registers 1817–1920, are in the series
Registers of General Correspondence (FO 566), and for the most part
record the arrival and handling of individual papers and dispatch of
replies. Each register for each country has an index, and copies of these
are available on microfilm in FO 605.

Foreign Office correspondence for the period 1906 to 1919 is covered by a card index in the Open Reading Room. From 1920 to 1951

the index is in the form of printed volumes, also held at the National Archives, and for the years 1952, 1953 and 1959 there are similar non-published departmental indexes also held in the Open Reading Room. These indexes mainly refer to papers in FO 371 Political Departments, but some refer to other departments, such as FO 369 Consular Department, FO 370 Library and Research Departments, FO 372 Treaty Department and FO 395 News Department. For the years 1954 to 1958 and 1960 to 1966 there are no detailed indexes in these series, and it is necessary to consult the relevant series lists to access the records. From 1967 to October 1968, when the Foreign and Commonwealth Office was formed, the political departments of the Foreign Office operated a common registry system with the Commonwealth Office and the Diplomatic Service Administration Office, and records from this period can be found in various FCO series by department.

7.1.3 Soldier resettlement records

One interesting class of emigrant were the army pensioners who were encouraged by the British and colonial governments to migrate to the colonies in the nineteenth century. These men were not necessarily old – in 1894 over half of army pensioners were under the age of 55. References to the settlement of some 8,000 ex-soldiers in Australia and New Zealand will be found in the *Alphabetical Guide to Certain War Office and Other Military Records (List and Index volume 53)*, under the name of the relevant colony. For visitors to the National Archives, this guide is kept behind the Research Enquiry desk.

The series WO 43 War Office: Secretary-at-War, Correspondence, Very Old Series (VOS) and Old Series (OS) 1809–57 contains papers relating to particular emigrant officers and soldiers in relation to half-pay, pensions, annuities and allowances. Similarly, you can find references to former soldiers who settled in any colony in WO 22 Royal Hospital Chelsea: Pensions Returns 1842–83. This series consists of periodical returns of pensions paid or payable by the Royal Hospital Chelsea, bound up in volumes and arranged under the various districts in the United Kingdom, Channel Islands, etc., and in India, the colonies and certain foreign stations. They include returns of out-pensioners of Chelsea and Greenwich Hospitals, of those belonging to the East India Company, and of mercantile marine pensioners; also annual mortality returns showing the number of deaths at different ages. In addition to the statistical information which these returns supply, they are useful for those trying to trace changes of residence and an individual pensioner's date of death.

The idea of soldier resettlement rose to prominence again during the First World War. By the end of the war all of the dominions had legislated to encourage immigration and in 1922 the Empire Settlement Act was passed. This led to the emigration of some 40,000 ex-soldiers, mainly to Canada. The resettlement schemes were generally considered to be a failure. Too few people joined up and those that did were left in an exposed position by the world industrial slump of the 1920s. They suffered financial ruin in their thousands, leaving dominion governments to carry the debts. Leaving the land, they became a new unemployed urban class in the dominions' major towns and cities. The only plus was the development of virgin land – few of the political objectives were achieved.

The soldier resettlement policy for this period largely resulted in the formation of the Overseas Settlement Committee, which was eventually taken over by the Overseas Settlement Board in 1925.

See the archives of the receiving countries for detailed archival sources, including case studies. Series relating to policy at the National Archives include CO 721 Overseas Settlement Department: Original Correspondence 1918–1925 and CO 532 Dominions Original Correspondence 1907–25. Relevant specific pieces include CAB 27/174 Overseas Settlement 1922 and CAB 37/144/75 Report of the Cabinet Committee on Land Settlement for Sailors and Soldiers 1916.

7.1.4   *Poor Law Union records*
From 1834 many poor emigrants were provided with assistance for the passage by their parish, under the provisions of the Poor Law Amendment Act. The records of the administration of this assistance in MH 12 can include lists of emigrants, giving their occupation and destination. Historically these records have long been inaccessible to researchers as they are, firstly, arranged chronologically by county and Poor Law Union, not by subject, and, secondly, rather voluminous. The National Archives is, however, working to improve access. The returns for the Poor Law Union of Southwell in Nottinghamshire, for example, can now be freely searched by first and last name(s), places mentioned, corporation name, occupation and free text such as 'emigration' on DocumentsOnline. The project is being extended to cover Poor Law Union records in another 20 counties across England and Wales, with the help of local volunteers. Similar records relating to parish-organized emigration will be found locally at appropriate county record offices.

MH 19 contains general correspondence relating to the Poor Law Board. Of the files in the series, which cover a wide range of topics, MH 19/22 is particularly relevant here. This relates specifically to passage-assisted emigration and includes lists of emigrant ships reported to have arrived in British territories between 1836 and 1876.

7.1.5   *Overseas Settlement Board*
In 1925, the Overseas Settlement Department and the Overseas Settlement Committee were transferred from the Colonial Office to the Dominions Office.

Correspondence of the Overseas Settlement Department is in DO 57 with registers in DO 5 and DO 6. Minutes of the meetings of the Overseas Settlement Board are in DO 114/89–90. The papers of W.B. Amery while British government representative in Australia for migration (1925–8) and principal, Overseas Settlement Department (1929–31) are in DO 190. Records of the CRO departments that dealt with the Overseas Migration Board are in the MIG series in DO 35 and DO 175.

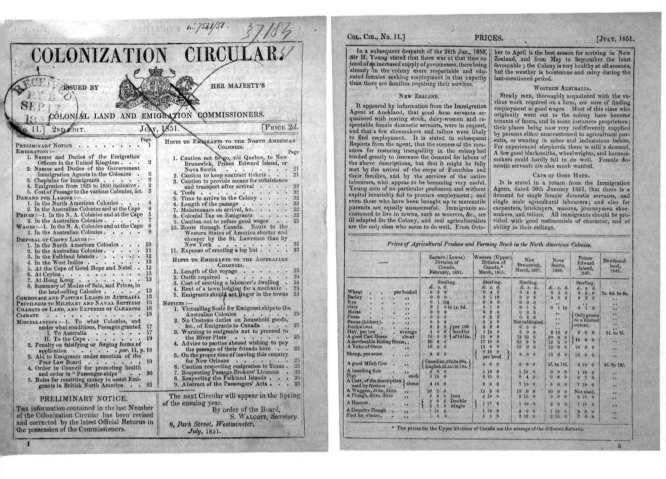

7.2 Migration to North America and the West Indies

The major early collection of papers relating to the West Indies and the American colonies is in the series CO 1. PROQuest (*www.proquest.com*) has produced a database of Colonial State Papers which provides access to thousands of papers concerning the American, Canadian, and West Indian colonies between the sixteenth and eighteenth centuries. All documents from CO 1, including maps, have been reproduced as high-quality, full-colour images digitized directly from the original documents.

It is also worth searching the following series of original correspondence for North America, together with related registers: CO 5 America and West Indies, Original Correspondence 1606–1822; CO 6 British North America Original Correspondence 1816–68; CO 42 Canada, formerly British North America, Original Correspondence 1700–1922; CO 60 British Columbia, Original Correspondence 1858–71; CO 188 New Brunswick Original Correspondence 1784–1867; CO 194 Newfoundland Original Correspondence 1696–1922; CO 217 Nova Scotia and Cape Breton Original Correspondence 1710–1867; CO 226 Prince Edward Island Original Correspondence 1769–1873; CO 326 General Registers 1633–1849; CO 327 British North America Emigration Registers 1850–63; CO 328 British North America General Registers (including emigration 1864–8); CO 329 British North America Registers of Out-letters 1872–80; PC 1 Privy Council and Privy Council Office: Miscellaneous Unbound Papers 1481–1946; PC 5 Privy Council Office: Plantation Books 1678–1806; SP 54 Secretaries of State: State Papers Scotland Series II 1688–1782 (for Scottish emigrants); and T 1 Treasury: Papers 1557–1920.

7.2.1 Company Records

The West New Jersey Society was a company formed about 1691 for the development of the 'Hereditary Government of West Jersey in America'. Tracts of land in West and East New Jersey, Pennsylvania, New England and elsewhere were divided into 1,600 parts, forming the shares of the adventurers. These on death fell to the heirs, executors or administrators of the deceased.

Records for the period 1658–1921 can be found in the series TS 12. These consist of original in-letters, entry books and drafts of out-letters, minute books of its court and committees, ledgers and accounts, registers of the transfer of shares, maps and plans, original deeds and charters, a history of the society, and miscellaneous papers relating to claims etc. of legal and historical importance.

Founded in 1670, the Hudson's Bay Company's (HBC) chief interests for its first two centuries were the fur trade, exploration and settlement. After 1870, when its territory of Rupert's Land was incorporated into the Dominion of Canada, its interests became more varied. The series BH 1 comprises the following eight types of records of the Hudson's Bay Company:

Headquarters records
Records concerning posts in North America
Logs, books and papers relating to ships in the company's service
Governors' papers
Miscellaneous records, which include correspondence and journals of various individuals, as well as records of the Red River Settlement (1811–90), Vancouver Island colony (1848–61), Arctic expeditions (1824–66), and the Parliamentary select committees
Records of allied and subsidiary companies, which include the North West Company (1786–1851), the Puget's Sound Agricultural

Company (1838–1932), the International Financial Society Ltd (1859–69), the Russian American Company (1821–1903), the Assiniboine Wool Company (1829–36), the Red River Tallow Company (1832–3), the Vancouver Island Steam Sawmill Company (1852–6), the Vancouver Coal Mining Company (1861–1900), and the Buffalo Wool Company (1822–4)

Western Department land records
Records from the Commissioner's Office in Winnipeg.

The series also includes manuscript and published maps, charts and plans of Hudson's Bay Company forts, coal mines, various American and British territories and Canadian cities and towns, together with architects' drawings, specifications and atlases.

The records in BH I are microfilm copies of original records held at:

The Hudson's Bay Company Archives (HBCA),
Provincial Archives of Manitoba
200 Vaughan Street, Winnipeg
Manitoba R3C 1T5
Canada

Tel: 204 945 4949
Website: *www.gov.mb.ca/chc/archives/hbca*

The HBCA website offers further information about the company's records and history.

7.2.2 *American Loyalist claims*

The peace treaty signed at the end of the American War of Independence in 1783 provided for a recommendation by the Congress of the United States for the restoration of the property of 'real British subjects'. This recommendation was intended to cover the claims of those Americans who had suffered losses during the war as a result of their loyalty to the Crown. And today the records that survive as a result of it provide an intriguing means of tracing British citizens who emigrated to the United States and fought on the Loyalist side.

In 1794 a new treaty, commonly known as Jay's Treaty, was signed between Great Britain and the United States. The sixth article of this treaty provided for the settlement of debts – an issue not addressed in 1783 – while the seventh article provided for the American merchants and citizens for loss of vessels and property during the war. When deadlock arose in the settlement of claims under the sixth article in 1799, the British government suspended its proceedings under the seventh article.

In 1802 a new convention was signed by the two countries for the mutual payment of claims. The board constituted under the seventh article of the treaty of 1794 resumed its work and the American government undertook to pay the sum of £600,000 in satisfaction of the money they might otherwise have been liable to pay under the terms of the sixth article.

Three commissioners were appointed in Britain under the Distribution of Certain Monies Act 1803 to deal with claims under this article in respect of outstanding debts from British merchants and from Americans who had remained loyal to the Crown.

Claims amounting to nearly £5 million were considered by these commissioners, of which £1,420,000 were accepted. Successful claimants received dividends pro rata from the money made available by the American government which, with interest, amounted to £659,493. The commission made its final adjudication on claims in 1811 and presented its last report to the Treasury in June 1812 when it wound up its proceedings.

You can find records of the claims for compensation of American citizens who suffered property losses through loyalty to the British Crown in AO 12 Audit Office: American Loyalist Claims Series I 1776–1812, AO 13 Audit Office: American Loyalist Claims Series II 1780–1835. These consist of entry books and ledgers containing the evidence of witnesses, reports and other communicated documents, the examinations and decisions of the commissioners, lists of claims, etc.

Researchers visiting the National Archives may consult in the Research Enquiries Room an index to names in AO 12 which precedes the standard list. In this index the person's name is followed by an abbreviation of the name of the state where the individual claimed to have suffered loss. A volume number and a further number follow these details. The volume number is the same as the piece number that can be found in the left-hand column of the list. For example: Ackerly, Isaac, N.Y., v23, 21; in this entry v23 translates into piece 23, and AO 12/23 is the reference to use when ordering the piece on the computer. The second number, 21, is an internal reference which should not be used when requesting the piece (it is the page number in the volume on which the information can be found). The page number in the document is the handwritten number; the printed numbers on the top right-hand corner are the folio numbers and do not correlate to the index.

Rolls of declared accounts from the Auditors of the Imprest and the Commissioners of Audit relating to Loyalist claims can be found in AO 1. Treasury papers should be consulted for papers concerning the claims and some compensation and pension lists of American Loyalist claims lodged under article 6 of the 1794 treaty of Amity. The series T 50 Pay Lists and other Documents concerning Refugees 1780–1856 and T 79 American Loyalist Claims Commission: Records, 1777–1841 contain the reports of commissioners investigating individual claims, and some compensation and pension lists.

7.2.3 Land grant records

In early colonial America, land ownership was considered to be vested in the king through the right of discovery and settlement by his subjects. The monarch in turn granted land to companies and to proprietors to organize settlements and also to some individual subjects as a reward for service.

The system whereby recipients of royal land grants in turn gave or sold land to others varied. In some colonies, notably New England, the legislatures set up by the colonists assumed jurisdiction over the allocation of company lands. They made some direct grants to individuals for 'adventuring' money in the companies, but the greater part went to groups or communities to establish townships and apportion the surrounding lands.

In the southern colonies the 'headright' system of land distribution was the most common method followed during the seventeenth century. By this grant an individual who provided transportation to the colony of any emigrant was entitled to at least 50 acres of land. During the same period, however, larger tracts were given by the king, proprietor or company to favourites, to those who performed outstanding service for a company, or, as in Maryland, to those who transported five or more persons to the colony. The 'headright' system led to many

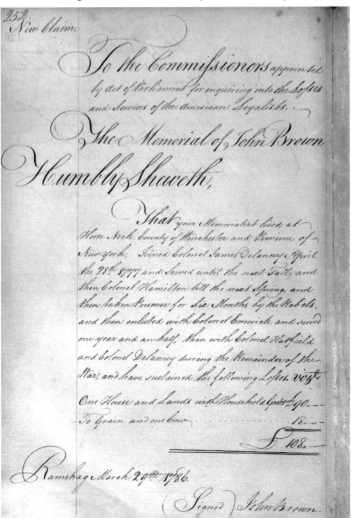

FIG. 33 *Memorial of John Brown for compensation for loss of property during the American War of Independence.*
AO 12/23

frauds and abuses and by the early years of the eighteenth century most of the land was distributed by purchase or by taking out a patent signed by the Governor of a colony for new unpatented land.

No systematic list or comprehensive index exists of the many varied land grants made in colonial America. C.M. Andrews in his *Guide to the Materials for American History to 1783 in the Public Record Office of Great Britain* (1912, 1914) gives references to the subject generally and to many individual grants. References to other grants can be obtained from the *Journals of the Board of Trade and Plantations, the Calendar of State Papers, Colonial, America and West Indies* and the *Acts of the Privy Council, Colonial Series*, all of which are available for consultation at the National Archives. Details of the grants referred to in the Journals can be found in the Colonial Office document series CO 5 America and West Indies, Original Correspondence. The records of a great many of the land grants made remained in the colonies and may be available in US State archives.

Sources for nineteenth-century land grants can be found in CO 6 North America: Original Correspondence 1816–68 and CO 384 Original Correspondence, Emigration 1817–96. Settlers in the nineteenth century, mainly British troops already stationed there, applied for land grants and CO 384/51 provides a list of North American settlers, giving personal details of age, career, marital status, children, purpose of application and signature of applicant. This record covers the period 1837–8.

See J.M. Kitzmuller, *In Search of the 'Forlorn Hope': a Comprehensive Guide to Locating British Regiments and their Records* (1988) to establish where regiments were stationed at particular times. This book is available at the Research Enquiries desk. Alternatively, you could consult the following series of records: WO 379 Office of the Commander-in-Chief and War Office: Adjutant General's Office: Disposition and Movement of Regiment, Returns and Papers (Regimental Records) 1737–1950; and WO 380 Office of the Commander-in-Chief and War Office: Adjutant General's Office: Designation, Establishments and Stations of Regiments, Returns and Papers (Regimental Records Series I–IV) 1803–1953. Both series record the location and movement of troops in regiments of the regular and Territorial Army in the United Kingdom, Ireland and overseas. They are thought to have been maintained by the Adjutant General's Office but latterly were kept in the Ministry of Defence library, where they were probably used to answer historical queries about British regiments.

Other sources include WO 17 Office of the Commander-in-Chief: Monthly Returns to the Adjutant General 1759–1865 and WO 73 Office of the Commander-in-Chief and War Office: Distribution of the Army Monthly Returns 1859–1950. Both series are summarized returns issued by the Quartermaster General, the Adjutant General and the Army Council. They show the distribution of the Army month by month: (a) by divisions and stations, and (b) by regiments in numerical order. They give the station of each battalion or company, the numbers of officers and rank and file present or absent and other statistical information.

Land grants relating to the West Indies are described in G. Grannum, *Tracing Your West Indian Ancestors* (1995). Examples of land grants survive for the following: the Bahamas (CO 23/3, 125); Belize (WO 55/1815); the Ceded Islands (CO 76/9, CO 101/1, 11, CO 106/9–12); Dominica (T 1/453); Grenada (CO 101/1); Guyana (CO 111/28, CO 116/73, 75–76); Jamaica (CO 137/28, 162); St Christopher (CO 152/13, T 1/275); St Vincent (T 1/453); Surinam (WO 1/149) and Trinidad (CO 295/35).

7.2.4 *Twentieth-century migrants*

One of the largest groups of migrants to the US and Canada in the twentieth century were Second World War brides. It is estimated that over a million US GIs (Government Issues) and Canadian servicemen were stationed in Britain during the Second World War, and that in excess of 80,000 British women became their war brides. Although there is no central complete listing of war brides, you can find entries for them among those of other emigrants in the Board of Trade outward passenger lists in BT 27 (see 1.2.4).

The printed indexes to the general correspondence of the Foreign Office (FO) also contain information relating to the passage of war brides to Canada and the US – because of tight immigration laws a special Act of Congress needed to be passed in the US in 1947 to facilitate their migration.

It is not clear how many babies were the products of wartime affairs that ended with the American and Canadian fathers shipping out of Britain; estimates range from 20,000 to 50,000. TRACE (Transatlantic Children's Enterprise) is a non-profit making self-help support group whose aim is to help people trace their GI/Canadian fathers/families. Information about TRACE can be found at *www.gitrace.org*.

7.3 Migration to Australia and New Zealand

British settlement of Australia began with the establishment of a penal colony at Botany Bay on the east coast of Australia in 1788, and prisoner transportation continued until 1857. Australia also, however, attracted free settlers, though there are relatively few records relating to voluntary migrants to Australia and New Zealand at the National Archives until the passenger lists (BT 27) begin in 1890. See 1.2.4 for the passenger lists. Transportation to the colonies is covered in chapter 8.

Aside from the general Colonial Office sources referred to in 7.1, CO 201 New South Wales Original Correspondence 1783–1900 includes lists of settlers, 1801–21. The correspondence of 1823–33 has also been indexed in a supplementary finding aid to this series, available in the Open Reading Room at the National Archives. CO 386 Land and Emigration Commission, etc. 1833–94, contains original correspondence and entry books of the Agent General for Emigration, the South Australian Commissioners and the Land and Emigration Commission.

Names of Australian settlers can also be traced in CO 202 New South Wales Entry Books 1786–1873; CO 360 New South Wales Register of Correspondence 1849–1900 and CO 368 New South Wales Register of Out-Letters 1873–1900. Few names, however, can be searched using the Catalogue for these series.

The censuses of New South Wales and Tasmania conducted at intervals between 1788 and 1859 are valuable sources. Although primarily conducted to record convict details, the censuses do include the names of individuals who 'came free' or who were 'born in the colony'. See 8.2.1 for more details.

The National Archives of Australia (NAA) website *www.naa.gov.au* holds records relating to Australia's schemes to sponsor British migrants prior to the Second World War and after. Such schemes included the 'Group Settlement' and 'Land Settlement' schemes, and the famous '£10 Pom' scheme. This scheme ran from 1950 to 1973 and selected case studies can be found at the National Library in Canberra. The Archives has committed to making records for the 7 million people who migrated to Australia searchable on the internet, in a project likely to take several years.

The Genealogical Society of Victoria has catalogues and microfiche collections relating to free, assisted and non-assisted immigration to Australia, with sources relating to settlement in Victoria (from 1835), New South Wales (from 1835), South Australia (from 1836), Tasmania (from 1804) and Northern Territory (from 1824).

New Zealand on the other hand was never used as a penal colony. Details of migrants may be found in CO 208 New Zealand Company Original Correspondence 1839–58. The New Zealand Company was formed in 1839 and incorporated in 1841 with power to buy, sell, settle and cultivate land in New Zealand. It surrendered its charter in 1850 and was dissolved in 1858. You can find registers of cabin passengers emigrating, 1839–50, in CO 208/269–72, applications for free passage, 1839–50, in CO 208/273–4 (indexed in CO 208/275), applications for land and lists of landowners, in CO 208/254–5. The series also contains lists of agents and surveyors, lists of German migrants and lists of maintained migrants.

Names of New Zealand settlers can be traced in CO 209 New Zealand Original Correspondence 1830–1922. The Genealogical Society of Victoria has various fiche collections relating to settlement in New Zealand from 1840 after British sovereignty was declared.

7.3.1 *Land purchases and free passages*

The very strict government regulations set for local agents when selecting migrants for free passages to New South Wales, Western Australia, Tasmania and New Zealand are detailed in CO 386/29. References to payments that covered migrants' travel expenses to their port of embarkation can be found in locally kept parish records.

The series CO 386 Land and Emigration Commission Papers 1833–94 contains documents relating to colonization of Australia through the Wakefield Scheme of 1829 (Fig. 35). This saw land sold for a substantial price in the colony, and the funds thus generated were used to ship emigrant labourers from Britain to work the land. Those purchasing the land were assured of an adequate supply of labour of the right type, since labourers were vetted before being given the passage. The labourer was promised a new and more prosperous life in a colony where labour was in demand, while prospects were poor at home. The scheme proposed to set up a colony along approved lines and at the same time relieve unemployment and pauperism at home.

The South Australian Colonization Commission, a predecessor of the Land and Emigration Commission, was responsible for laying down the regulations for land sales and overseeing the selection of emigrants eligible for a free passage.

FIG. 34 *Registers of cabin passengers emigrating to New Zealand aboard the* Bolton. CO 208/269

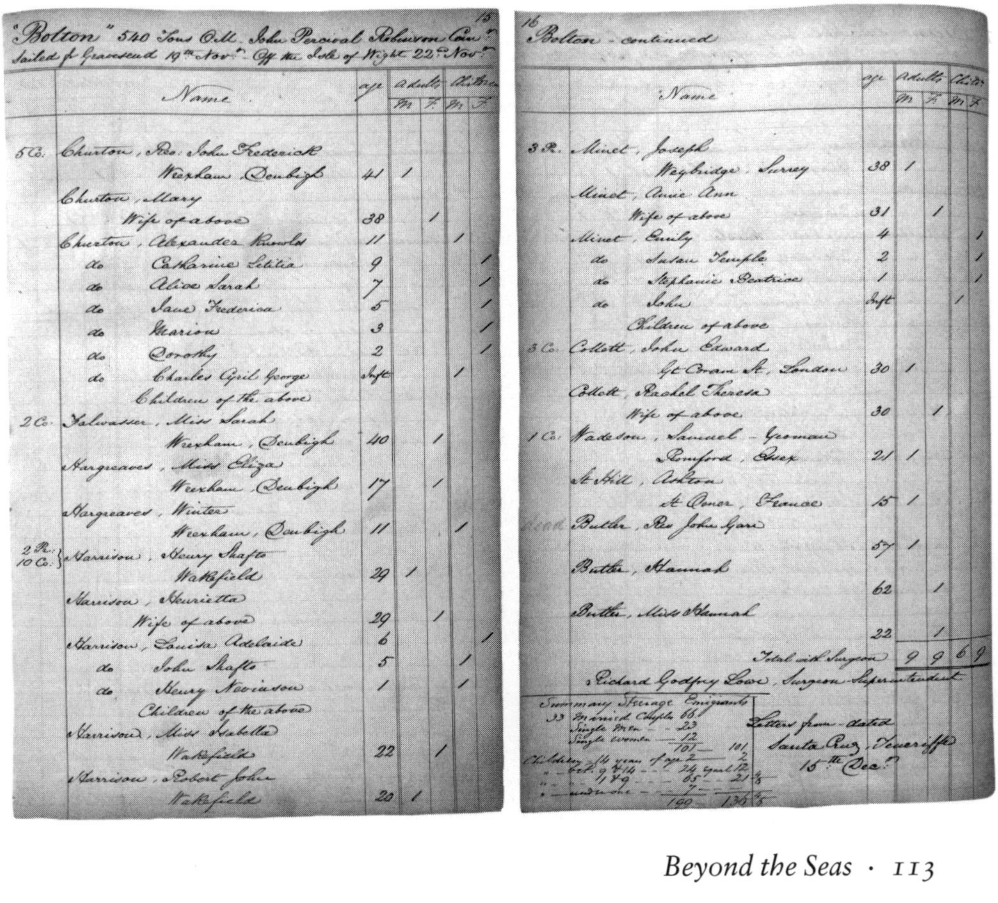

15

"Bolton" 540 Tons O.M. John Percival Robinson Comr.
Sailed fr Gravesend 19th Novr. Off the Isle of Wight 22d Novr.

	Name	Age	Adults M	Adults F	Children M	Children F
5 Co.	Churton, Revd. John Frederick, Wrexham Denbigh	41	1			
	Churton, Mary, Wife of above	38		1		
	Churton, Alexander Knowles	11			1	
	do Catharine Letitia	9				1
	do Alice Sarah	7				1
	do Jane Frederica	5				1
	do Marion	3				1
	do Dorothy	2				1
	do Charles Cyril George	Inft			1	
	Children of the above					
2 Co.	Falwasser, Miss Sarah, Wrexham, Denbigh	40		1		
	Hargreaves, Miss Eliza, Wrexham Denbigh	17		1		
	Hargreaves, Winter, Wrexham, Denbigh	11			1	
2 R. 10 Co.	Harrison, Henry Shafto, Wakefield	29	1			
	Harrison, Henrietta, Wife of above	29		1		
	Harrison, Louisa Adelaide	6				1
	do John Shafto	5			1	
	do Henry Newinson	1			1	
	Children of the above					
	Harrison, Miss Isabella, Wakefield	22		1		
	Harrison, Robert John, Wakefield	20	1			

16

Bolton – continued

	Name	Age	Adults M	Adults F	Children M	Children F
3 R.	Minet, Joseph, Weybridge, Surrey	38	1			
	Minet, Annie Ann, Wife of above	31		1		
	Minet, Emily	4				1
	do Susan Temple	2				1
	do Stephanie Beatrice	1				1
	do John	Inft			1	
	Children of above					
3 Co.	Collett, John Edward, Gt Ormond St, London	30	1			
	Collett, Rachel Theresa, Wife of above	30		1		
1 Co.	Wadeson, Samuel – Yeoman, Romford, Essex	21	1			
	St Hill, Ashton, St Omer, France	15	1			
	Butler, Revd John Gare	57	1			
	Butler, Hannah	62		1		
	Butler, Miss Hannah	22		1		
	Total with Surgeon		9	9	6	9

Richard Godfrey Lowe, Surgeon Superintendent

Summary Steerage Emigrants
33 Married Couples 66
Single Men – 23
Single women – 12
101 – 101
Children 14 years of age 2 – 2
" – bet. 9 & 14 – 24 equal 12
" – 1 & 9 – 65 – 21 2/3
" – under one – 7 –
199 – 136 2/3

Letters from – dated
Santa Cruz, Teneriffe
15th Decr.

The documents CO 386/142–3, 145–6 and 148–52 contain information relating to the Wakefield Scheme, the South Australian Colonization Commission, the sale of land in Australia to individuals and labourers' applications for free passages.

7.3.2 Army pensioners

Between 1846 and 1851, Army pensioners were encouraged to settle in New South Wales and New Zealand, although many of them failed as settlers.

Reference to ex-soldier emigrants to Australia, 1830–48, can be found in WO 43/542. Pension return records for District Offices survive for New South Wales, 1849–80, in WO 22/272–5; for South Australia,

FIG. 35 *A record of sale of land in 1839 under the Wakefield Scheme.* CO 386/146

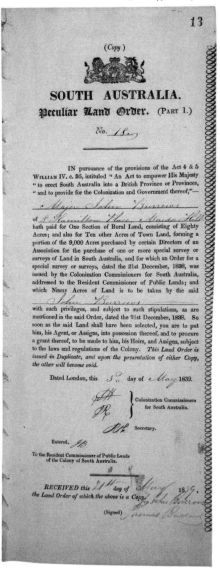

Queensland, Tasmania and Victoria, 1876–80, in WO 22/227, 297, 298 and 300.

See WO 43/543 for New Zealand returns. You can find those for 1845–54 and 1875–80 in WO 22/276–93.

7.4 Migration to South Africa

After some dispute as to ownership of the Cape of Good Hope between colonial powers, the territory was recaptured by the British from the Dutch in 1806 and formally became a British colony in 1814. In 1843 Natal was declared a British colony, and by 1902 Britain had gained control of the former Boer republics of the Orange Free State and Transvaal. In 1910 Cape Colony, Orange River Colony, Natal and Transvaal united to form the new Union of South Africa. All provinces attracted British settlers.

The series CO 48 Cape of Good Hope Colony (Cape Colony), Original Correspondence 1807–1910 contains letters from settlers and papers about grants of land at the Cape of Good Hope, 1814–25. Those interested in this colony should also see CO 49 Cape of Good Hope Colony (Cape Colony) Entry Books 1795–1872, CO 336 Cape of Good Hope (Cape Colony) Register of Correspondence 1850–1910 and CO 462 Cape of Good Hope (Cape Colony) Register of Out-letters 1872–1910. All series contain references to individual settlers, though these are not indexed by name of settler on the Catalogue.

There are two excellent published works relating to British settlers in South Africa: P. Philip, B*ritish Residents at the Cape, 1795–1819* (1981) and E. Bull, *Aided Immigration from Britain to South Africa, 1857–1867* (1991). Both contain lists of settlers compiled using original sources and provide information relating to particular nineteenth-cen-tury emigration schemes, such as the Byrne Settlers who came to Natal from all over the UK.

Individual files on immigrants after 1910, when South Africa became the Union of South Africa, are available via the Department of Home Affairs in South Africa:

Department of Home Affairs
Private Bag X114
Pretoria, 0001
South Africa

The series WO 148 Civilian Claims to Military Compensation Boards, South African War 1900–05 contains a representative selection of registers, indexes, and files relating to claims made by civilians to the Central and District Military Compensation Boards in respect of losses suffered by reason of the South African War, or for property that had been requisitioned by the military forces.

Registers of payments to Army and Navy pensioners (including some widows and orphans) at the Cape of Good Hope and elsewhere in South Africa, 1849–58 and 1876–80, are in WO 22/243–4. The muster rolls of the Cape Levies, 1851–3, may prove useful (WO 13/3718–25).

7.5 Migration to India

The India Office Records at the British Library are the ideal place to start for those researching family history with an Indian connection prior to independence. These records comprise the archives of the East India Company (1600–1858), of the Board of Control or Board of Commissioners for the Affairs of India (1784–1858), of the India Office (1858–1947), of the Burma Office (1937–1948) and of a number of related British agencies overseas.

The digitization of a card index that was compiled for a portion of these records in the 1970s means that some 300,000 births, baptisms, marriages and deaths can now be researched along with biographical details on the British Library's website.

An excellent collection of material relating to emigration to India, including birth, marriage and death announcements (and obituaries) extracted from Indian newspapers, can be found at:

The Society of Genealogists
14 Charterhouse Buildings
Goswell Road
London
EC1M 7BA

Website: *www.sog.org.uk*

7.5.1 Company and society records
The East India Company was established in 1600 as a joint-stock association of English merchants who received, by a series of charters, exclusive rights to trade to the East Indies. The East Indies were defined as the lands lying between the Cape of Good Hope and the Straits of Magellan, and the Company soon established a network of warehouses or 'factories' throughout south and east Asia. Over a period of 250 years the Company underwent several substantial changes in its basic character and functions.

Rivalry between the Old and New Companies after 1698 resulted in the formation in 1709 of the United Company of Merchants Trading to the East Indies. This 'new' East India Company was transformed during the second half of the eighteenth century from a mainly commercial body with scattered Asian trading interests into a major territorial power in India with its headquarters in Calcutta. The political implications of this development eventually caused the British government in 1784 to institute standing Commissioners (the Board of Control) in London to exercise supervision over the Company's Indian policies. This change in the Company's status, along with other factors, led to the Acts of Parliament of 1813 and 1833 which opened British trade with the East Indies to all shipping and resulted in the Company's complete withdrawal from its commercial functions. The Company continued to exercise responsibility, under the supervision of the Board, for the government of India until the reorganization of 1858.

With the India Act of 1858 a single new department of state, the India Office, replaced the Company and the Board of Control. This functioned, under the Secretary of State for India, as an executive office of United Kingdom government alongside the Foreign Office, Colonial Office, Home Office and War Office. The Secretary of State was assisted by a statutory body of advisers, the Council of India, and headed a staff of civil servants organized into a system of departments largely taken over from the East India Company and Board of Control establishments, and housed in a new India Office building in Whitehall. The Secretary of State for India inherited all the executive functions previously carried out by the Company, and all the powers of 'superintendence, direction and control' over the British government in India previously exercised by the Board of Control.

Improved communications with India via overland and submarine telegraph cables (1868–70) and the opening of the Suez Canal (1869) rendered this control, exercised through the Viceroy and provincial Governors, more effective in the last quarter of the nineteenth century. It was only with the constitutional reforms initiated during the First World War, and carried forward by the India Acts of 1919 and 1935, that there came about a significant relaxation of India Office supervision over the Government of India, and with it, in India, a gradual devolution of authority to legislative bodies and local governments. The same administrative reforms also led in 1937 to the separation of Burma from India and the creation in London of the Burma Office. Both the India Office and the Burma Office were dissolved following the grant of independence to India and Pakistan in 1947, and to Burma in 1948.

As indicated above, the British Library holds the vast majority of East India Company records. It is therefore best to begin your research at the India Office Records biographical index *http://indiafamily.bl.uk/ UI/Home.aspx*.

The European Manuscripts collection of the India Office Library houses the private papers of several hundred people who served in India, including Viceroys and Governors, civil servants, army officers and other ranks, businessmen, missionaries, scholars, travellers and their families. This growing collection (now over 16,000 volumes) of letters, diaries, papers of all kinds and tape-recordings supplements the official records and illustrates the wide diversity of work and social life in India and neighbouring countries since 1650.

The National Archives holds the series of records FO 41 General Correspondence before 1906, East India Company 1776–97, which consists of correspondence with the Court of Directors of the East India Company. Also available at the National Archives is the series CO 77 East Indies Original Correspondence, Entry Books 1570–1856. This series contains original correspondence and entries relating to the East Indies and includes documents relating to Persia and China, and to the embassy to China of 1793 to 1794.

The *Calendar of State Papers East Indies, 1513–1668* includes material available at both the British Library and the National Archives. Copies of the calendars are available in the Open Reading Room.

The Asia, Pacific and Africa Collections contain extensive records of India for both the period 1600 to 1858, when the East India Company controlled the region, and from 1858 to 1947, when India was ruled by the British government through the India Office. Among the numerous sources there is a card index with details of nearly 300,000 civil and military personnel, their families and others. The collections also contain registers of births, marriages and burials, arranged by presidency (Bengal, Bombay, Madras), registered wills of the three presidencies, railway employees, and service records for military personnel in the East India Company and the Indian Army.

See L/AG/46/4, L/AG/46/10–12 and L/AG/46/18 for records of appointments in the United Kingdom to employment in Indian Railway Companies 1848–1925. There is a separate card index in the Reading Room for these records.

The National Archives Library collection holds a run of the annual *East India Register*, continued by the *India List* (under various titles) from 1791 to 1947, as well as the separate *Indian Army Lists*.

7.5.2 *Indian Army records*

Personal records relating to the Queen's India Cadetships 1858–1930 (L/MIL/9/292–302), Sandhurst cadets commissioned into the Indian Army Unattached List 1859–1940 (L/MIL/9/303–19) and Quetta cadets 1915–18 (L/MIL/9/320–32) can all be found in the Asia, Pacific and Africa Collection. Also available at the Asia, Pacific and Africa Collection are assistant surgeons and surgeons' papers 1804–1914 (L/MIL/9/358–408).

See I.A. Baxter, *Brief Guide to Bibliographical Sources in the India Office Library* for records of service for officers, surgeons, departmental warrant officers, NCOs and privates. For officers of the Bengal Army 1758–1834, see V.C.P. Hodson, *List of the Officers of the Bengal Army* (1927–47). For surgeons, see D.G. Crawford, *Roll of the Indian Medical*

Service 1615–1930 (1930). A run of the annual Indian Army Lists available at the National Archives provides potted histories of officers.

7.5.3 Indian civil service records

These records are also available at the British Library and include an incomplete series of writers' petitions, 1749–1856, and appointment papers for East India Company civil servants with baptismal certificates and educational testimonials. Brief service records for high-rank-ing civil servants appear in the *India Office List 1886–1947* in the Reading Room.

Histories of service (v/12 series) for higher-ranking officers from 1879 give promotions and postings, sometimes dates of birth. Civil lists (v/13 series) for lower-rank officials from 1840 do not give a continuous career record, and researchers consequently need to consult a sequence of annual volumes to establish an individual's career.

Records of personnel employed in government railways, police, public works, post office, etc., 1818–1900, 1922–8, can be found in L/F/10 series. Name, occupation, salary and period of residence in India are usually provided in these records. Deaths in the Uncovenanted Civil Service 1870–1949 are to be found in L/AG/34/14A. These records give name of deceased, date and place of death, rank, age, native town and country, next of kin and custody of property (if any). There is a separate card index in the Reading Room.

As with army records, you could also consult the East India Register, continued by the *India List* (under various titles) from 1791 to 1947.

7.6 Migration to the Middle East

7.6.1 The Levant Company records

The Levant Company was established in 1581 when its members were granted a monopoly of English trade with the Turkish Empire. Its representative at the Turkish court at Constantinople was also given diplomatic authority as English ambassador. Subsequently, consulates, manned by representatives of the Company, were appointed at strategic trading posts throughout the western Turkish Empire, including Aleppo, Algiers, Cairo, Chios, Patras, Salonika, Smyrna, Tunis and Zante.

By the second half of the eighteenth century, the Levant Company was in financial difficulties and could no longer afford to maintain the ambassador and consuls without government subsidy. In 1804, the Foreign Office took over full responsibility for the British embassy at Constantinople and the Company appointed its own consul general to look after its commercial interests.

The consuls enforced the ordinances of the company throughout the Levant, levied consulage on imports and exports, maintained law and order, adjudicated disputes, administered the estates of Englishmen who died abroad and exercised control over the factors who were the local representatives of merchants based in London. Large factories, such as in Aleppo, also appointed a salaried treasurer and a chancellor, who recorded all the official business of the factory and registered all acts, contracts and wills made by the factors.

The series SP 105 Secretaries of State: State Papers Foreign, Archives of British Legations 1568–1871 consists of letter books and correspondence of British embassies and legations abroad, mainly to the year 1796. It includes records of the Levant Company's London-based governing body, the General Court, and its officers, including minute books of the General Court (1611 to 1706), letter books of instructions to ambassadors, consuls and other agents (1606 to 1825) and treasurer's accounts. Of the Company diplomatic and consular missions, only Constantinople, Aleppo, Smyrna and Cairo are represented.

Amongst the miscellaneous records of British envoys, agents and ambassadors are the letter books of Sir Balthasar Gerbier, minister at Brussels (1631 to 1642); correspondence of the commissioners appointed to oversee the demolition of the fortifications of Dunkirk under the terms of the treaty of Utrecht; letter books of the Secretary of State concerning peace negotiations at Utrecht (1711 to 1714); letter books of missions involved in peace negotiations with France (1698 to 1772) and missions to the Imperial Diet and states within the Holy Roman Empire.

Also included are the collections of the correspondence and papers of individual diplomats – notably Sir George Stepney (1663 to 1707) concerning his missions to German states and the Holy Roman Empire and Sir Joseph Williamson (1633 to 1701) and Sir Leoline Jenkins (1623 to 1685) concerning their negotiations at the congresses of Cologne (1673) and Nimeguen (1676). Correspondence of the resident minister at the court of Tuscany includes dispatches from the government agent Philip von Stosch concerning the movements of the Old Pretender and the Jacobite court.

Levant Company out-letter books to 1670 are described in the Calendar of State Papers (Domestic Series) of the reign of Charles II; these are available for consultation in the Map and Large Document Room.

7.6.2 *The British mandate in the Middle East*

Between 1920 and 1948, Palestine was administered by the United Kingdom under a League of Nations (later United Nations) mandate. For most of this time, the mandate territories were run by a Government of Palestine, which employed local residents and, especially in the police service, the railways and port authority, UK and Commonwealth citizens. Many of these built up pension entitlements, which after the end of the mandate became the responsibility of the Colonial Office.

Administration and payment of the pensions passed to the Crown

Agents and then to the Department for Technical Co-operation. The records used to administer the pensions are now held by the Department for International Development, Abercrombie House, Eaglesham Road, East Kilbride, Glasgow G75 8EA, which still administers the pensions. After the end of the mandate, a trust fund set up to provide for the dependants of those killed or wounded by terrorist action in Palestine was administered by a committee for which the Colonial Office provided the secretary.

Included among the other territories of the former German and Ottoman Empires, given under mandate by the League of Nations to the Allied Powers to administer, was Iraq. For records relating to this mandate see CO 696 Iraq: Sessional papers, 1917–31, CO 730 Iraq: Original Correspondence 1921–32 and CO 781 Iraq: Register of Correspondence 1921–32. The remaining mandates were in Africa, in the Cameroons and Tanganyika.

8 ENFORCED MIGRATION

Throughout history, people have been forced to move from one place to another. Often, this has been for reasons of economic hardship or political persecution, as discussed in chapter 4 for example. But it has also been for other reasons. Unique to Britain was a policy of transportation – a system that exiled convicts to certain British colonies for a period of years (normally varying from seven years to fourteen years) during which time the convict would be forced to work productively and thereby learn new habits of industry and self-discipline and at the same time benefit the development of the colonial economy. The home government did not consider transportation as a matter of simply dumping human refuse on the colonies – it was genuinely thought to be effective, efficient and humane. Those who were transported were often quite young: it was, after all, the young who were most likely to benefit from a new life in a new world, and who were most likely to be fit enough to supply the productive labour that the new world needed.

The colonial authorities, not unnaturally, tended to take a more jaundiced view of the benefits of transportation, and many resented it. As a result of an order by the Privy Council, it became increasingly common for a pardon to be offered to convicts who had been sentenced to death, on condition of transportation overseas. In 1718 an Act of Parliament (4 Geo. I c.11) standardized transportation to America at 14 years for those who had been sentenced to death and introduced a new penalty – transportation for seven years – as a sentence in its own right for a range of non-capital offences. Transportation to America ceased in 1776 because of the outbreak of the American War of Independence. It was reinstated in 1787 to Australia and Van Diemen's Land (Tasmania) from 1803. Transportation lasted until 1857, when it was effectively abolished, though the Home Secretary retained the right to impose transportation until 1868. In total, over 220,000 men and women were transported between 1615 and 1868.

In parallel, Britain also operated a unique enforced child emigration policy, mainly for child paupers, from as early as 1618 to as late as 1967. It has been estimated that some 150,000 children were sent to the British colonies and dominions during this period, most notably America, Australia and Canada, but also Rhodesia, New Zealand,

South Africa and the Caribbean. Many of the children were in the care of the voluntary organizations who arranged for their emigration. Child emigration peaked from the 1870s until 1914, and some 80,000 children were sent to Canada alone during this period. The vast majority would never return to Britain.

The aim of child emigration was often to increase the population within the colonies, and to improve labour and productivity there. Although most schemes were presented as being for the benefit and the welfare of the children, few schemes actually took the feelings of the children into account.

8.1 Transportation to America and the West Indies, 1615–1776

It is probable that some 50,000 men, women and children were transported to America and the West Indies between 1615 and 1776. Most were from the poorest class and nearly half received their sentences from courts in or around London. It should, however, be noted that transportation to the West Indies was, right from the start, for a period of no more than 10 years, as most of the islands forbade longer sentences. Although the majority of cases of transportation to the West Indies took place during the period 1615–60, between 1824 and 1853 some 9,000 convicts were sent from Britain to help build the naval and military station at Ireland Island, Bermuda.

8.1.1 Printed sources
Much useful information relating to transportation to America and the West Indies has been printed. Probably the most concise book is P.W. Coldham, *The Complete Book of Emigrants, 1607–1776* (1988), which, using central and local sources, lists names of those transported together with the month and year of sentence – sufficient to locate surviving court records. Other information provided includes occupation, month of embarkation and landing, name of ship and destination.

8.1.2 Trial records
Convicts transported between 1615 and 1718, or transported for 14 years after 1718, would have been convicted in a court of assizes or one with equivalent legal power. Surviving assize court records are normally held at the National Archives. Transcripts of trials do not normally survive, but gaol books, indictments or depositions can usually be traced. Trials that took place in the Central Criminal Court Old Bailey, 1674–1913, are now available online at *www.oldbaileyonline.org*. This is fully searchable and contains nearly 200,000 criminal trials.

Convicts may also have been tried at the Quarter Sessions, the records of which are held in local record offices. It should be noted that not all those who were sentenced to transportation actually went. Some convicts were successful in an application for mercy. Before 1784, reference to such applications may be found among State Papers (SP), Domestic Records. *The Calendars of Home Office Papers, George III, 1760–1775*, in the Map and Large Document Room at the National Archives, include lists of criminals, with information relating to the crime committed, sentence passed and the date and location of criminal trial. Original records to which the calendars refer can be found in SP 44 State Papers: Entry Books 1661–1828.

8.1.3   *Pardons, appeals and petitions*

The series of records SP 35 Secretaries of State: State Papers Domestic, George I and SP 36 Secretaries of State: State Papers Domestic, George II contain a large and miscellaneous collection of papers concerning transportation to America. Included here are letters of appeal from convicted prisoners, their friends and families, lists of reprieved felons and opinions of judges. *Calendars of Home Office Papers, George III, 1760–1775*, in the Map and Large Document Room, include lists of criminals, with information relating to the crime committed, the date and location of criminal trial and the sentence passed. *Calendars of State Papers, Colonial, America and West Indies, 1574–1738*, are available in the Open Reading Room at the National Archives. A CD-Rom version is also available on OPERA in the Reading Rooms.

C 66 Chancery and Supreme Court of Judicature, a series of parliament rolls written in Latin, contains a complete series of pardons from the death penalty, on condition of transportation, from 1654 to 1717.

8.1.4   *Transportation lists*

The T 1 Treasury Papers series includes a mass of transportation lists, starting in 1747 and ending in 1772. *Calendars of Treasury Papers, 1557–1728, Treasury Books, 1600–1718*, and *Treasury Books and Papers, 1729–1745*, are available in the Open Reading Room. The series T 53 Treasury: Entry Books of Warrants relating to the Payment of Money includes records of payment made by the Treasury to contractors engaged in the transportation of felons from 1718. Until 1744 the names of all those to be transported from the City of London and the home counties, together with the names of the ships in which they were to be transported, and the destination American colony, are included in the Money Books. Thereafter, only statistics concerning transported felons are entered, together with the names of the transporting ships and their masters.

CO 5 Board of Trade and Secretaries of State: America and West Indies, Original Correspondence 1606–1822 includes material on all aspects relating to transportation to America and the West Indies. A key finding aid to this series is *Calendars of State Papers, Colonial, America and West Indies, 1574–1738*, available in the Open Reading Room at the National Archives. A CD-Rom version is also available on OPERA in the Reading Rooms.

8.2 Transportation to Australia, 1787–1868

Following the outbreak of the American War of Independence in 1776, transportation to America ceased to be an option for the British government. Sentences of transportation were still passed, but convicts were held in prison instead. Naturally, these soon became overcrowded, a problem that was only partially solved by the introduction of extra accommodation in the form of ships (prison 'hulks') moored in coastal waters. The solution to the crisis was to develop a new penal colony, and in 1787 the 'First Fleet' of 11 ships set sail to establish a new penal colony at Botany Bay on the east coast of Australia. A second fleet followed in 1790 and a third left in 1791.

It is estimated that over 1,000 ships transported in excess of 165,000 men, women and children to Australia and Van Diemen's Land (Tasmania) between 1787 and 1867. In the 1830s, 4,000 people were being transported every year. Although transportation had effectively come to an end by 1857 and had become increasingly unusual well before that date, it is estimated that a further 9,500 male convicts were sent to Western Australia between 1860 and 1868, when the practice was finally abolished.

8.2.1 *Printed and online sources*

A great detail of useful information relating to transportation to Australia has been printed. Details of convicts who sailed on the early fleets have been published in such books as P.G. Fidlon and R.J. Ryan (eds), *1788: The First Fleeters* (1981), D. Chapman, *People of the First Fleet* (1981), M. Gillen, *The Founders of Australia: A Biographical Dictionary of the First Fleet* (1989), M. Flynn, *The Second Fleet: Britain's grim convict armada of 1790* (1989) and R.J. Ryan, *The Third Fleeters* (1983). A dedicated website for the First Fleet is available at *http://firstfleet. uow.edu.au/index.html*.

For later years, you can find names of convicts and settlers on the published censuses for the penal colonies, the most complete being the census of New South Wales in November 1828. Edited by M.R. Sainty and K.A. Johnson, this census was published in 1980 by the Library of Australian History. The original records of the 1828 census are available on microfilm at the National Archives in the series HO 10.

Aside from *www.oldbaileyonline.org*, many local archives have developed databases of convicts tried locally who were known to have been transported to Australia. These include:

www.lancastercastle.com for Lancaster Castle records

http://microsites.lincolnshire.gov.uk/archives/section.asp?catid=6722
for transportation of convicts from Lincoln assizes
http://freepages.genealogy.rootsweb.ancestry.com/~jdriver/news/Trans portations.html for transportation of convicts from Nottingham assizes
http://freepages.genealogy.rootsweb.ancestry.com/~mrawson/ses-sions.html for transportation of convicts from Kent assizes
www.yorkfamilyhistory.org.uk/assizes.htm for transportation of convicts from York assizes.

Finally, for convicts transported to New South Wales, you should check the website of the State Records New South Wales (*www.records. nsw.gov.au/archives/indexes_online_3357.asp#Convicts*). These include indexes to:

Certificates of freedom, 1823–69
Tickets of Exemption from Government Labour, 1827–32
Bench of Magistrates, 1788–1825
Colonial Secretary correspondence, including letters, land grants, tickets of occupation, memorials, petitions, etc., 1788–1825.

Records of convicts transported from Ireland, 1791–1853, are available at the National Archives of Ireland. These include prisoners' petitions and cases 1788–1836 and transportation registers, 1836–57, which can be searched by name of convict at *www.nationalarchives.ie/ search/index.php?category=18*. Unfortunately, all transportation registers compiled before 1836 were destroyed in the Four Courts fire of June 1922. Therefore, if the person you are researching was convicted before 1836, but was not the subject of a petition, he or she will not appear on this database. Other databases relating to Irish convicts can be searched at *http://members.pcug.org.au/~ppmay/convicts.htm*. As most of these convicts were transported to West Australia, the following site entitled NSW Convict Women may be of interest:

http://members.iinet.net.au/~perthdps/convicts/confem.html

For convicts transported to Van Diemen's Land (Tasmania) between 1804 and 1853, check the following site:

http://portal.archives.tas.gov.au/menu.aspx?search=11

8.2.2 *Trial records*
As with America, surviving records of assize trials are held at the National Archives. The assize records are not indexed by personal name; instead, they are arranged by assize circuit, and then by record type. To find a particular case, you must know the name of the accused,

the county or circuit where they were tried and the approximate date of the trial. For the nineteenth century, if you do not know where or when the accused was tried, you can look at the Annual Criminal Registers, for England and Wales 1805–92 in HO 27 or for Middlesex 1791–1849 in HO 26 Criminal Registers. An incomplete name index to HO 27, arranged by county and then by name within, is available on microfiche.

The series HO 26 and HO 27 both list those charged with indictable offences, giving place of trial, verdict and sentence. Once you have this information, check the various series of records for criminal assizes held in English and Welsh assizes. Survival of assize records is patchy, as the clerks of assize, who kept them, tended to destroy them when they became too bulky to store. If a suitable record exists for the year and place in question, go to the series list of the series indicated. See local record offices for records of trials at courts of Quarter Sessions.

Criminal trial records are very formal; they do not normally contain either transcripts of evidence or any information about age and family relationships. In addition, the information given about occupation and residence is rarely accurate.

If you really want good quality personal information about a convict, then you would be better advised to look for an application for clemency. Because people asking for clemency or a pardon wanted to prove that they were worthy of mercy, they often included a lot of information designed to establish how respectable they were and this would include just the kind of details about personal circumstances and family background that family historians want to know.

8.2.3 *Pardons, appeals and petitions*
The series HO 17 Criminal Petitions, Series I 1819–39 (Fig. 36) and HO 18 Home Office: Criminal Petitions, Series II 1839–54 are arranged in coded bundles so you will need to use the registers in HO 19 to identify the right one. The registers are arranged by the date of receipt of the petition. They date back to 1797 and include information about the response to the petition, so you can sometimes find out something useful about a convict even if the petition itself does not survive. Currently, the catalogue for HO 17 is being indexed by name, though this may take some time to complete. Until then, the registers in HO 19 need to be consulted.

You can also find petitions in HO 48 Law Officers' Reports, Opinions and Correspondence 1782–1871, HO 49 Law Officers' Letter Books 1762–1871, HO 54 Civil Petitions and Addresses 1783–1854 and HO 56 Petitions Entry Books 1784–1922. These records, however, are not indexed.

The series HO 47 Judges' Reports on Criminals 1784–1829, searchable by name on the Catalogue, and HO 6 Judges' and Recorders' Returns 1816–40 are also informative. These sometimes include unofficial transcripts of evidence and comments on the characters of both witnesses and juries as well as memorials and petitions from friends and relatives of the accused. The *Calendars of Home Office Papers, George III, 1760–1775*, in the Map and Large Document Room also include Judges' Reports on Criminals.

Wives could accompany their convict husbands, and a number applied to do so. Surviving petitions can be found in PC 1 Privy Council and Privy Council Office: Miscellaneous Unbound Papers, notably PC 1/67–92 for 1819–44, and in HO 12 Criminal Department: Old Criminal (OC) Papers for 1849–71. HO 12 references can be identified via HO 14 Criminal Department: Registers of Papers 1849–70. CO 201 New South Wales Original Correspondence 1783–1900 and CO 386 Colonial Office: Land and Emigration Commission, etc. 1833–94 include letters from people wishing to join convict relatives. For example, CO 386/154 consists of a register of applications for passages to the colonies for convicts' families, 1848–73.

8.2.4 Transportation lists

You can find the name of the ship on which the convict sailed as well as the date and place of conviction and the term of the sentence for the dates 1787–1870 in HO 11 (Fig. 37). The contents of these records have been used in the compilation of the British Convict Transportation Registers 1787–1867 database, which is now available at *www.slq.qld.gov.au/ info/fh/convicts*. This allows you to search details for over 123,000 of the estimated 160,000 convicts transported to Australia.

ADM 101 Office of the Director General of the Medical Department of the Navy and predecessors: Medical Journals, 1785–1963 includes surgeons' journals from convict ships and emigrant ships (1817–56), for which naval surgeons were provided. The National Archives was awarded a grant by the Wellcome Foundation to produce a full catalogue description of these journals for the period 1793–1880 (1,178 journals in total). The journals contain accounts of the treatment of medical and surgical cases, and usually a copy of the daily sick list, statistical abstracts of the incidence of diseases, and general comments on the health and activities of the ship's company. These records are an extremely important source of information on shipboard health, as well as being of great interest to family historians, and have the bonus of providing fascinating insights into living conditions, climate, culture and the environment in places where ships docked. Similar journals can be found in MT 32 Admiralty Transport Department, Surgeon Superintendents' Journals of Convict Ships 1858–67.

The series PC 1 Privy Council and Privy Council Office: Miscellaneous Unbound Papers 1481–1946 and PC 2 Privy Council: Registers 1540–1978 contain additional material about transportation. The latter, for example, contains lists of convicts transported for 14 years or less. TS 18/460–525 and TS 18/1308–61 include contracts with agents

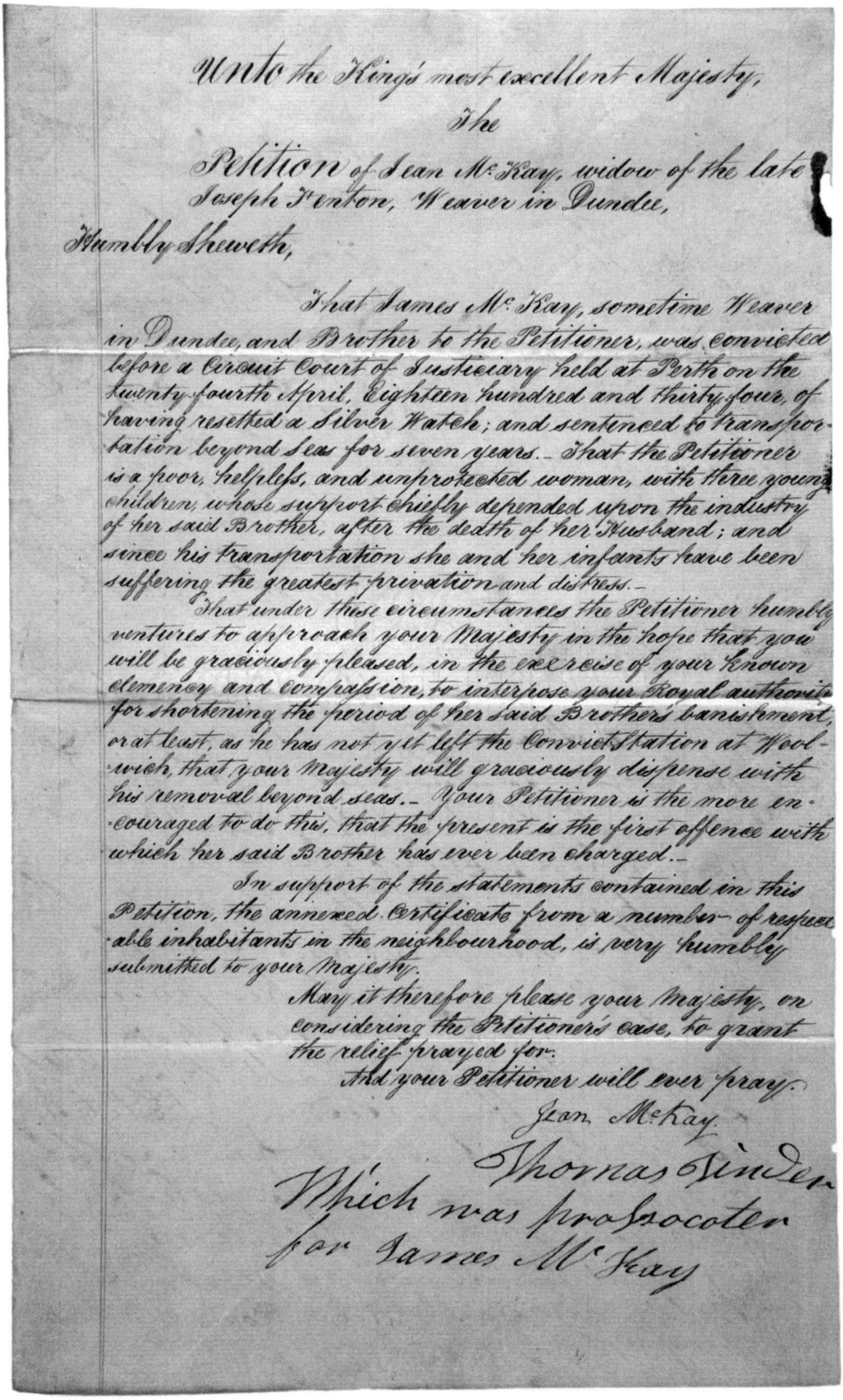

FIG. 36 *A petition
for the release of
James Mackay,
sentenced to
transportation in
April 1834.*
HO 17/22

Unto the King's most excellent Majesty,

the

Petition of Jean McKay, widow of the late
Joseph Fenton, Weaver in Dundee,

Humbly Sheweth,

That James McKay, sometime Weaver
in Dundee, and Brother to the Petitioner, was convicted
before a Circuit Court of Justiciary held at Perth on the
twenty-fourth April, Eighteen hundred and thirty-four, of
having resetted a Silver Watch; and sentenced to transportation beyond Seas for seven years. — That the Petitioner
is a poor, helpless, and unprotected woman, with three young
children, whose support chiefly depended upon the industry
of her said Brother, after the death of her Husband; and
since his transportation she and her infants have been
suffering the greatest privation and distress. —

That under these circumstances the Petitioner humbly
ventures to approach your Majesty in the hope that you
will be graciously pleased, in the exercise of your known
clemency and compassion, to interpose your Royal authority
for shortening the period of her said Brother's banishment,
or at least, as he has not yet left the Convict Station at Wool-
wich, that your Majesty will graciously dispense with
his removal beyond seas. — Your Petitioner is the more encouraged to do this, that the present is the first offence with
which her said Brother has ever been charged. —

In support of the statements contained in this
Petition, the annexed Certificate from a number of respectable inhabitants in the neighbourhood, is very humbly
submitted to your Majesty.

May it therefore please your Majesty, on
considering the Petitioner's case, to grant
the relief prayed for.

And your Petitioner will ever pray.

Jean McKay.

Thomas Linden
Which was prosecutor
for James McKay

to transport the prisoners, with full lists of ships and convicts for the period 1842–67.

Records of those awaiting transportation in prison hulks (ship prisons) are also available at the National Archives. HO 8 Home Office: Convict Prisons: Quarterly Returns of Prisoners 1821–76 consists of sworn lists of convicts on board the hulks and in convict prisons with particulars as to their ages, convictions and sentences, health and behaviour.

8.2.5 *Settlement in Australia*

As mentioned in 8.2.1, many websites and published material exist for convicts who settled in Australia. Original documents at the National Archives include CO 201 Colonial Office and Predecessors: New South Wales Original Correspondence 1783–1900. This series contains lists of convicts for Norfolk Island, an island 1,670 kilometres northeast of

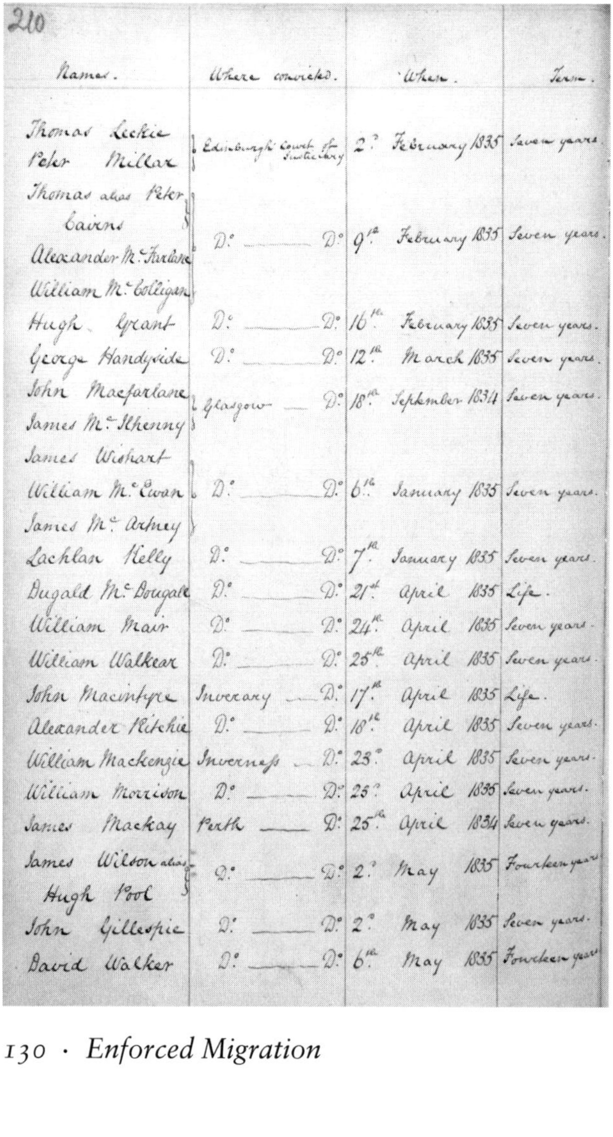

210

Names.	Where convicted.	When.	Term.
Thomas Leckie Peter Millar	Edinburgh Court of Justiciary	2d February 1835	Seven years.
Thomas alias Peter Cairns Alexander McFarlane William McColligan	D° ——— D°	9th February 1835	Seven years.
Hugh Grant	D° ——— D°	16th February 1835	Seven years.
George Handyside	D° ——— D°	12th March 1835	Seven years.
John Macfarlane James McIlhenny	Glasgow ——— D°	18th September 1834	Seven years.
James Wishart William McEwan James McArthney	D° ——— D°	6th January 1835	Seven years.
Lachlan Kelly	D° ——— D°	7th January 1835	Seven years.
Dugald McDougall	D° ——— D°	21st April 1835	Life.
William Mair	D° ——— D°	24th April 1835	Seven years.
William Walkear	D° ——— D°	25th April 1835	Seven years.
John Macintyre	Inverary ——— D°	17th April 1835	Life.
Alexander Ritchie	D° ——— D°	18th April 1835	Seven years.
William Mackenzie	Inverness ——— D°	23d April 1835	Seven years.
William Morrison	D° ——— D°	25d April 1835	Seven years.
James Mackay	Perth ——— D°	25th April 1834	Seven years.
James Wilson alias Hugh Pool	D° ——— D°	2d May 1835	Fourteen years
John Gillespie	D° ——— D°	2d May 1835	Seven years.
David Walker	D° ——— D°	6th May 1835	Fourteen years

FIG. 37 *A list of those transported to Australia in 1835 including James Mackay.* HO 11/10

the east Sydney coast of Australia. Papers relating to convicts in New South Wales and Tasmania in HO 10 contain material relating to convicts' pardons and tickets of leave from New South Wales and Tasmania, 1835–59. HO 7/2 includes information about deaths of convicts in New South Wales in the brief period 1829–34.

Lists of convicts and emigrants who settled in Australia between 1801 and 1821 can be found together in CO 201. Names can also be traced in CO 202 New South Wales Entry Books 1786–1823, CO 360 New South Wales Register of Correspondence 1849–1900 and CO 369 New South Wales Register of Out-Letters 1873–1900. Records of the superintendent of convicts in New South Wales, 1788–1825, are held in the State Archives of New South Wales (*www.records.nsw.gov.au*). Some of the lists from these records have been printed in L.L. Robson, *The Convict Settlers of Australia*.

8.3   Child Migration Schemes

Records of child migrants are scattered among private and public archives around the globe.

8.3.1   *Home Office and Poor Law Union records*

Before 1972, responsibility for the application of various acts relating to children lay with the Home Office. The series of records MH 102 consists of policy and correspondence files in the Home Office. Related policy files in the CHN (Children) series, which originated in the Home Office in 1949, can be found in BN 29 and BN 62, with representative case files in BN 28. The vast majority are closed for 75 years, though it is possible following the prompts on the Catalogue to request a review of the information from closed material under the Freedom of Information Act 2000. Earlier files can be found in general series of Home Office registered papers in HO 45 and HO 144. Mainly policy and correspondence files relating to the migration of children under the Children Act 1908, ch. 67, the records include schemes for the migration of children to Canada and Australia.

In terms of emigration specifically, the files contain material relating to schemes set up by the UK, South Africa, Canada, New Zealand and Australia between 1910 and 1960. Records include movements set up by Dr Barnardo's and Barnardo's Homes, the Fairbridge Society, the Overseas Migration Board and the Big Brother migration scheme. A small number of representative personnel files are closed for 75 or 100 years. Again, by following the prompts on the Catalogue it is possible to request a review of the information from closed material under the Freedom of Information Act 2000.

Sadly, few series of the National Archives documents record individual details of child migrants. For example, Local Government Board

Poor Law records in the series MH 12 tend to record only statistical information on the numbers of children sent overseas from individual Poor Law Unions, though they do sometimes include Poor Law Union posters giving notice of the names and ages of children being sent abroad.

MH 19 contains both the incoming and outgoing correspondence and papers of the Poor Law Commission and Board and the Local Government Board for the period 1834–1909 and the Second World War. The records are arranged by names of corresponding departments, and registers of correspondence are in MH 20.

The series covers a wide range of subjects, from public health to Poor Law administration. It contains a significant amount of material relating to child emigration, of which MH 19/9 is particularly interesting.

FIG. 38 *Pauper children in the Poor Law Union of Poplar earmarked for emigration in 1884.* MH 12/7698

POPLAR UNION.
DESERTED CHILDREN

NOTICE IS HEREBY GIVEN that, on the 12th day of December next, the Guardians of the Poor of the Poplar Union will proceed to consider the question of the expediency of assisting the

EMIGRATION TO CANADA

Of such of the following children as may be then maintained in the District or other School chargeable to this Union by reason of their having been deserted, or otherwise abandoned, by their Parents, and who by age, physical capacity and otherwise may then be found to be eligible for such emigration, namely:--

NAMES.	Ages	NAMES.	Ages
BYFORD, WILLIAM	11	HAGERTY, ELLEN	11
„ FREDERICK	9	HEWSON, GEORGE	11
BROWNING, SAMUEL	7	„ JOSEPH	10
„ FREDERICK	5	HODGE, EVA	8
BERRY, ALFRED	12	MAKER, GEORGE	5
„ FREDERICK	8	„ ELIZABETH	4
BRIGHTWELL, ELIZABETH	11	MEREDITH, EMMA	10
BROWN, DOLLY	12	„ „ CHARLES	8
BRIAN, JAMES	9	„ „ WALTER	7
„ MARY	6	MONK, MARY ANN	11
„ PATRICK	1	„ ELIZA	9
BRITTAIN, ADA	9	„ RACHEL	6
„ „ CHARLES	3	MARTIN, FREDERICK	8
„ „ WILLIAM	2	„ HENRY	7
BOLTON, BERTIE	5	„ AMELIA	4
„ EDITH	8	NEWBERRY, ALBERT	11
CAVERLEY, ARCHIBALD	10	„ WILLIAM	9
CRAWLEY, ANN MARY	13	OLDING, SUSAN	7
CALLAGHAN, MARGARET	9	OXHALL, RICHARD	5
„ ELLEN	6	„ EDWARD	3
DEELY, LOUISA	4	PRATT, ROBERT	9
ELLICK, SARAH	16	ROWBOTHAM, WILLIAM	5
„ LOUISA	14	SOUTH, CATHERINE	11
HOLMES, CHARLOTTE	12	„ GEORGE	8
„ JANE	9	SHERVILLE, PERCY	8
HAMILTON, ARTHUR JOHN	11	SHACHL, ALBERT	11
„ „ WILLIAM	7	SILK, HARRIET	10
„ „ GEORGE	4	WHITWROWE, JENNIE	4
HARVEY, RICHARD	10	WHITE, AGNES	12
„ „ GEORGE	6	„ MARGARET	4
„ „ MARGARET	2	WILLIAMS, JOHN	11
HUGHES, ALBERT	13	WARD, MARY ANN	14
„ „ FANNY	12	WILKINSON, THOMAS	11
HANCOCK, ALICE	12	„ „ SARAH	10
„ „ ARTHUR	10	„ „ HENRY	6
„ „ HERBERT	8	WILLMOTT, JEFFREY	10
„ „ ALBERT	5	„ „ SARAH	4
„ „ OLIVE	3		
„ „ HENRY	1		

BY ORDER,
JAMES R. COLLINS, Clerk.

Union Offices: High Street, Poplar.
September 12th, 1884.

This document provides detailed reports on pauper child emigrants sent to Canada between 1887 and 1892. The reports, compiled by the Secretary Department of Agriculture on instruction from the Dominion of Canada Immigration Officer, give comments about their condition, health, character, schooling, frequency of church attendance and about each child's view of their new homes. The reports cite the Union or parish from which each child was sent, as well as giving their name and age, and host's name and address. Further Canadian government inspectors' reports and statistical information regarding child migrants can be found in Parliamentary Papers, copies of which are available on microfiche in the Open Reading Room at the National Archives.

8.3.2 Children's Overseas Reception Board (CORB) records

Probably the richest source of material on child migrants at the National Archives are records concerning the Children's Overseas Reception Board (CORB). This was set up in 1940 in response to enemy bombing raids on British cities. The majority of CORB files were destroyed under statute in 1959. However, the administrative files in DO 131 survive, including a selection of case files relating to children (DO 131/94–105) and their escorts (DO 131/71–87) and registers of child applicants (DO 131/106–12), which provide history cards for the 2,664 children evacuated overseas. Details include full name of child, date and place of birth, parents' name, address in the UK, next of kin details, religious denomination, occupation (of parent), placement overseas (name and

FIG. 39 *A party of CORB children and their escorts en route to New Zealand in 1940.* DO 131/15

addresses), medical reports, school reports (if any) and further employment (if any). These records are searchable by name and date of birth of child on the Catalogue. Dominions Office policy files relating to the activities of the Board are available to consult in DO 35.

8.3.3   Outgoing passenger lists

The passenger lists digitized in partnership with findmypast (*www.find mypast.com*) are a useful source for child migrants who left ports in the United Kingdom and Ireland for final destinations outside Europe and the Mediterranean between 1890 and 1960. At *www.ancestry.co.uk* you can find details of child migrants bound for Canada, Australia, New Zealand and South Africa, such as their full name, age and, from 1922, a UK address. A person search using the first and last name can be refined by departure port, destination country, destination port and name of ship. See 1.1.3 and 1.2.4 for further details.

8.3.4   Local Record Offices in the UK

Local record offices throughout England and Wales hold Poor Law Union papers and Board of Guardian records that can provide detailed information relating to child migrants. For example, within the Greenwich Board of Guardians papers at the London Metropolitan Archives are papers relating to child migration to Canada from c.1907 to 1920 (LMA ref: GBG 218/1–238). These papers contain details of orphans and pauper children who were sent to Canada through a number of agencies, including the Salvation Army, the Catholic Church and various children's homes. For further information on records held in local archives in England and Wales, see the A2A database at *www.national archives.gov.uk/a2a*. This database contains catalogues describing archives held locally in England and Wales dating from the eighth century to the present day. At the time of going to press, the database holds 10.3 million records that relate to 9.45 million items held in 418 record offices and other repositories. For contact details of these repositories, go to *www.nationalarchives.gov.uk/archon*. The ARCHON Directory includes contact details for record repositories in the United Kingdom and also for institutions elsewhere in the world that have substantial collections of manuscripts.

8.3.5   University of Liverpool

The Department of Special Collections and Archives at the University of Liverpool (*http://sca.lib.liv.ac.uk/collections*) holds the archives of the Fairbridge Society as well as those of the National Children's Homes (now NCH Action for Children) and Barnardo's. The archives are subject to access restrictions. Records of individuals are normally closed for 100 years.

FIG. 40 *Dr. Thomas Barnardo.*
COPY 1/492

8.3.6 *Barnardo's Archives*

The Barnardo's Archives (*www.barnardos.org.uk*) hold numerous case histories of former residents and admission and discharge registers. Dating back to 1874, the archive contains 500,000 images and 300 films of the visual history of the organization, including its work overseas in Canada and Australia. The archive handles some 2,000 requests annually, searching photographs of former residents and responding to the needs of the media, publishers, photographic/film archive researchers and historians. Former residents have also donated prints and films, as well as their memories. The child migrant index at *www.barnardos. org.uk/what_we_do/work_with_former_barnardos_children.htm* holds files of some 30,000 Barnardo children who migrated to Canada, together with records of the MacPherson Homes and Marchmont Homes between the years 1882 and 1939. The latter acted as clearing houses for children sent overseas for adoption. There are restrictions on access. In general, access to the index and Barnardo's records is limited to proven descendants only.

8.3.7 *Catholic Children's Society Archives*

The Catholic Children's Society Archives, 73 St Charles Square, London, W10 6EJ, holds records relating to its homes and migration schemes to both Canada and Australia. Although records of individuals are normally closed for 100 years, a number of more general sources are open. These include a database of children who went overseas during the period 1938–63; a complete collection of registers of Catholic workhouse children, 1870–1920; admission and discharge registers for its homes at St Charles School, Brentwood, 1872–1950, St Nicholas' Industrial School and North Hyde School; Minute Books, 1897–1975; Annual Reports, 1904–65; and copies of the *St Peter's Net*, 1898–1973. The latter was the official newsletter of the Crusade of Rescue and Homes for Destitute Catholic Children.

8.3.8 *The Child Migrants Trust*
The Child Migrants Trust was established in 1987 by Nottingham social worker Margaret Humphreys to help former child migrants find their relatives. The Trust is able to conduct family research to locate relatives and to provide social workers to perform the delicate task of counselling and making the first contacts:

The Child Migrants Trust
28A Musters Road
West Bridgford
Nottingham
NG2 7PL

Tel: 0115 982 2811
Fax: 0115 981 7168
Website: *www.childmigrantstrust.com*

8.3.9 *Canadian records*
Between 1869 and the early 1930s Canada received over 100,000 child migrants from the UK. Canada's National Archives holds much relevant material and an increasing amount is available via its website at *www.collectionscanada.gc.ca.*

The original incoming passenger lists in the series RG 76 from 1865 to 1935 contain information such as passenger full name, age, country of origin, occupation and intended final destination. They are arranged by port and date of arrival, with the exception of some years between 1919 and 1924, when manifests were replaced by an individual form (Form 30A) for each migrant. Information on these forms includes name of ship, date of sailing, port and date of arrival, name, age, occupation, birthplace, race, citizenship, religion, destination and the name of the nearest relative in the country from which the immigrant came.

The entire collection of lists from 1865 to 1935 is available to search and download (for a fee) at *www.ancestry.ca.* For the years 1925 to 1935, the Immigration Records Database is available online at *www.collectionscanada.ca/archivianet/020118_e.html.* This site provides details of passengers and full references to the original passenger lists. The site is free to search.

Records of immigrants arriving at Canadian ports from 1 January 1936 onwards remain in the custody of Citizenship and Immigration

Canada. To request a copy of another person's immigration record, you should write to:

Citizenship and Immigration Canada
Public Rights Administration
360 Laurier Avenue West
10th Floor
Ottawa
Ontario
KIA ILI

According to the website requests can be submitted by Canadian citizens, permanent residents of Canada, Canadian Corporations or people present in Canada. The request should include the full name at time of entry into Canada, date of birth and year of entry. Additional information is helpful, such as country of birth, port of entry and names of accompanying family members.

The request must be accompanied by a signed consent from the person concerned or proof that he/she has been deceased for 20 years. Proof of death can be a copy of a death record, a newspaper obituary or a photograph of the gravestone showing name and death date. Proof of death is not required if the person would be over 110 years of age. See *www.cic.gc.ca/english/department/atip/factsheet.asp* for more details.

Members of the British Isles Family History Society of Greater Ottawa are currently indexing the names of British child migrants from the incoming passenger lists. The database can be searched online at *www.collectionscanada.gc.ca/databases/home-children/index-e.html* and covers the period 1869 to 1930, during which over 100,000 children were sent to Canada from the UK.

There are also records of the Immigration Branch Central Registry, which corresponded closely with the various sending agencies, including Dr Barnardo's, and its records are preserved in the series RG 76 BIA. These include annual reports, information booklets and some lists of names of children for the years from 1892 to approximately 1946. Similarly, Juvenile Inspection Reports are available in RG 76 C4C. These are essentially inspection reports carried out by immigration officials of children brought to Canada by various organizations in the 1920s, although there are a few records dated as early as 1914 and some as late as the 1930s. There is usually one page per child, with the following details: name, age or date of birth, year of arrival, name of ship, sending organization and names and addresses of the families with whom they were placed.

Library and Archives Canada (LAC) also holds microfilm copies of the records of the Middlemore Homes organization, which sent more than 5,000 young child migrants, aged between 2 and 18, mainly from Birmingham in the UK, to Canada between 1873 and 1936. Volunteers with the British Isles Family History Society of Greater Ottawa (BIFHSGO) are currently compiling an index for those records. If you locate an entry in that index, BIFHSGO will provide you with the specific archival references so that you can borrow the relevant microfilm reels from LAC or order copies of pages. The index can be accessed at *www.bifhsgo.ca/home_children_emigration_scheme.htm*.

LAC also hold, in the series RG 9, details of hosts and children who were evacuated before and during the Second World War. These total over 7,000 cases and are not just confined to CORB children.

8.3.10 *Australian records*

The National Archives of Australia collection covers almost 200 years of Australian history. Included among this collection are records relating to the policy of child migration, together with records relating to the service organizations and churches who sponsored the children, provided for their education and placement, and arranged their after-care, as well as individual case histories.

The range of papers usually found in migrant selection documents includes application forms, medical reports and other papers completed by applicants for assisted migration to Australia from the UK. Consolidated, they contain a wide range of personal details. In the case of child migrants, the application was usually completed by a guardian and the

FIG. 41 *A leaflet promoting the 'Big Brother' emigration scheme .* BT 298/410

associated forms would usually have such items as birth certificates, school reports, maintenance guarantees and even police character reports attached to them. These documents may also have the name of the particular organization that sponsored the migration, such as Barnardo's, the Christian Brothers or the Fairbridge Society. The majority of these records are arranged chronologically by date of ship arrival in Australia so it is important to have the name of the ship, the approximate date of arrival and the state in which the person arrived, otherwise a search may be time consuming with little guarantee of success.

Passenger records, which include passenger lists and passenger cards, provide a rich source of family history information. Each vessel arriving at the Australian ports was required to lodge a list of incoming passengers. Arranged by date and port of arrival, passenger lists include the name of each passenger and, in earlier lists, such details as age or marital status. There are no name indexes to these records, so date and port of arrival are critical for success. Passenger lists survive for all Australian ports from 1924, with some gaps. Some ports have lists dating from before 1924, such as Fremantle where lists start in the 1880s.

Records relating to child migrants – including migrant selection documents, passenger lists and immigration policy files – are held by the various state archives, details of which are available at the website for the National Archives of Australia (*www.naa.gov.uk*).

The Personal History Index (PHIND) database has been developed by the Christian Brothers, the Sisters of Mercy and the Sisters of Nazareth in Western Australia. It records the location of records held by a variety of institutions in Western Australia concerning child migrants who were cared for in that state by the three participating organizations. Information recorded on the database includes:

Name
Date and place of birth
Parents' names (if known)
Age at departure from the United Kingdom
Shipping details
Name and location of sending order in the United Kingdom
Destination order in Western Australia
Initial residence, as well as any transfers between homes and schools
Location of records on the subject, including medical, social,
    educational, baptismal, and immigration records – as well as
    sources of any records available in the United Kingdom.

A copy of this database is held by the National Archives in Perth. Access to PHIND is primarily for former child migrants and their families.

You can also consult the database www.cberss.org, which lists the location of records held in Australia for the 3,000 children resident in orphanages managed by the Christian Brothers, the Sisters of Mercy, and the Poor Sisters of Nazareth between 1938 and 1965.

The Barnardo's After Care section at *www.barnardos.org.au* provides a search facility for child migrants who were brought to Australia under Barnardo's schemes. The records consist primarily of a card index of all Barnardo migrants who came to Australia. Information on the card index includes name, date of birth, ship name and date of arrival, and any placement within New South Wales. The After Care Section can also retrieve the individual case records which are held in the Mitchell Library in Sydney. Access to these records is restricted to the surviving child migrant or their immediate next of kin only.

8.4   Case Study

8.4.1   *Eva and Hilda Rowe*

Eva and Hilda Rowe were sisters born in 1898 and 1902 respectively. They were committed on 26 November 1907 under 4 Edward V11 ch. 15 at the Southampton Petty Sessions Court. According to the Home Office report covering their case, the girls' father had twice been charged with neglect in the aftermath of his wife's death in 1905. On the last of these the girls were assessed as having 'undergone the severest of privations' and he had been sentenced to six months hard labour.

The children were put into the care of Dr Barnardo's Girls School in Barkingside and in January 1911 were selected for emigration to Canada, initially to reside at Margaret Cox's Girls Home, Peterborough, Ontario, Canada. This move was judged to be in the girls 'best interest'. Their father, however, raised an immediate objection. Living in Southampton, he felt that they were far enough away from him already and informed the school that 'if there are any means of stopping it [the emigration] I shall do so'.

Despite the intervention of their father, Eva and Hilda Rowe left London on the SS *Sicilian* bound for Quebec on 29 June 1911. It was unlikely that they would ever see him again.

Records relating to Eva and Hilda Rowe:

> BT 27/724 Outward passenger lists (London), June and July 1911 (including the list for SS *Sicilian*, 29 June 1911) – available at *www.ancestorsonboard.com*.
>
> HO 144/1118/203442 Children: Emigration of girls to Canada from Dr Barnardo's Homes, 1911–15.

9 MOVEMENTS WITHIN BRITAIN

Britain has increasingly had a mobile population, especially since the industrialization of the nineteenth century when railway and canal construction transformed the way people, British citizens and immigrants, lived their lives, socially and economically. There are a number of record series that can be consulted to trace different mobile communities. The sources listed below, such as Home Office papers, census returns, Poor Law correspondence, soldiers' documents and seamen's records can be used to find communities of British people moving on, as well as those of different national and ethnic groups. The Irish in particular, for economic reasons, are well represented in these records.

Aside from official records, there are an increasing number of online visual sources to illustrate the movement of people across Britain and indeed the globe. Developed by a team of geographers from University College London, the site *www.publicprofiler.org/worldnames* maps global surnames to help people find the origins of their name and how far it may have spread. The Public Profiler site plots 10.8 million last names using data from electoral rolls and phone directories. The site covers a billion people in 26 countries, showing the origins of names and where families have scattered. Similarly, using data from the UK censuses, *The British 19th Century Surname Atlas* is a fully interactive CD-ROM product that allows you to plot distribution maps for all of the surnames and forenames found in the 1881 census of England, Scotland and Wales. The programme can be searched by name.

9.1 Census Returns

The decennial census records for 1841–1901 for England and Wales can be consulted free online and on microform at Kew and on the internet at *www.nationalarchives.gov.uk/census*. You can search online by county, parish, surname, forenames and also by birthplace (and by address for the 1901 returns). The 1841 census recorded whether the respondent was born in the part of the country in which they were now resident. In terms of birthplace it asked whether an individual was born in Scotland, Ireland or 'Foreign parts'. From 1851 onwards, however, censuses recorded actual birthplace and the following type of information:

Address
Name and surname of residents
Relation of each person to head of household
Age of residents
Rank, profession or occupation
Birthplace
Whether blind or deaf and dumb.

This remained fairly standard for the following six censuses. In many cases place of birth outside the UK will simply be given as a country, but sometimes the county or state or city is also recorded. If you cannot find a family located in the same area, other areas with known immigrant communities should be searched. These communities had close ties and tended to stick together. Newly arrived immigrants would follow in the footsteps of former neighbours and friends from Ireland, for example, and often settle in the same area.

9.1.1 *The 1911 Census*
The census returns are hugely valuable in terms of what they can tell us about our ancestors, and the 1911 returns will reveal even more, as these are the original census returns filled out by the householder, as opposed to the enumerator. One of the key benefits, apart from seeing entries written in your ancestor's own hand, is that extra information is often included such as date of naturalization. The 1911 returns is being gradually made available from early 2009. A full unredacted version of the 1911 census will be available in January 2012.

9.2 Poor Law Records

MH 12, Correspondence with Poor Law Unions and other Local Authorities, contains papers concerning the whole field of Poor Law and (after 1871) local government and public health administration. These records include workhouse correspondence and poor law relief funds. The records are arranged alphabetically by county and union, so to find papers relating to a particular municipal borough or other local authority it is necessary to know in which Poor Law Union it was situated (see below). Registers to this correspondence have not survived, but indexes of selected subjects dealt with in the correspondence can be found in MH 15 Subject Indexes of Correspondence.

FIG. 42 *Census return from 1901 for Spitalfields showing numerous migrants and their families. RG 13/299*

A town or parish can be looked for in the 1851 census index under the county and the registration district given. The Poor Law Unions were used as the basis of civil registration districts in 1837, so the registration district given on a birth, marriage or death certificate or in the

No. of Schedule	ROAD, STREET, &c., and No. or NAME of HOUSE	HOUSES Inhabited	Uninhabited In Occupation	Not in Occupation	Building	No. of rooms occupied if less than five	Name and Surname of each Person	RELATION to Head of Family	Condition as to Marriage	Age (Males)	Age (Females)	PROFESSION OR OCCUPATION	Employer, Worker, or Own account	If Working at Home	WHERE BORN
137	3 Eastmans Court						Emanuel Bach	Son	S	17		Confectioner Baker	own account		Poland (Russian Subj)
							Martha Bach	dau	S	14		Confectioner	own account		Poland (Russian Subj)
							Leah do	dau	S		12				Poland (Russian Subj)
							Isaac Goldman	Uncle	M	36		Carman			Poland (Russian Subj)
							Israel Strapleski	Visitor	M	28		Ship assistant	worker		Poland (Austrian Subj)
							Annie Goldman	Servant	S		18	General Servant (domestic)			London Spitalfields
138	4 Eastmans Court	1					Henry Lee	Head	M	28		Costermonger	own account		London St George
							Helena Lee	Wife	M		25	Costermonger Hawks			London Stepney
							Barnard Lee	Son	S	5					London St George E
							Adelaide do	dau	S		3				London Spitalfields
							Kate Callahan	Son-in-law	S		20	Servant domestic		at home	London Whitechapel
139	5 do	1					Sarah Bernstein	Head	M		49	Costermonger Hawk	own account		Poland (Russian Subj)
							Myer do	Son	S	23		Costermonger Hawk	worker		London City
							Harry do	Son-in-law	S	21		Boot Paster	worker		London City
							Joseph do	Son	S	19		Enamel Worker	worker		London City
							Hadassah do	dau	S		17	Shirt embroiderer	worker		London City
							Leah do	dau	S		15	Shirt machinist	worker		London City
							Louis Bernstein	Son	S	13					London Spitalfields
							Rachel do	dau	S		11				London Spitalfields
140	6 Eastmans Ct	1					Abraham Cohen	Head	M	50		Costermonger (Drapery)	own account		Poland (Russian Subj)
							Esther Cohen	Wife	M		54				Poland (Russian Subj)
							Annie do	dau	S		19	Tailoress	worker		Poland (Russian Sub)
							Samuel do	Son	S	15		Cabinet maker	worker		London Spitalfields
							Simon do	G. Son	S	3					London Spitalfields
141	7 do	1					Isaac Aarons	Head	M	48		Cigar maker tobacco	worker		London White
							Solomon do	Son	S	21		Shop assistant	worker		London Spitalfields
							Betsy do	Wife	M		50				Holland
							Rosetta do	dau	S		15	Leather Curler	worker		London Spitalfields
142	8 do	1					Abraham Barnett	Head	M	50		Cigar maker tobacco	worker		London
							Sarah Barnett	Wife	M		47				London
	Total of Schedules 5	5							Total of Males and of Females...	16	14				

Note.—Draw your pen through such words of the headings as are inapplicable.

indexes at Kew will show you in which Union an event took place. Records of the Unions themselves, the boards of guardians and individual workhouses, where they survive, will be held locally; see J. Gibson, *Poor Law Union Records* (1993), available at The National Archives. These records are useful to trace families who were paid by the Poor Law Union to move to other parts of the country for economic reasons.

As mentioned in 7.1.4, records in MH 12 are hard to access. The National Archives is, however, committed to improving access and has embarked on a project to digitize them. Those for Southwell are now searchable on DocumentsOnline.

9.3 Soldiers' Documents

WO 97 Royal Hospital Chelsea: Soldiers Service Documents for non-commissioned officers and other ranks discharged up to 1913 contains the service records, attestation papers, medical records and discharge documents of many men who served in the British Army. The records are particularly useful in tracking where soldiers were recruited, with which regiment and where they served for the duration of their careers. Though many Irish soldiers were recruited in Ireland and after service returned there, others were recruited in England and settled here after they were discharged.

For soldiers who were discharged between 1760 and 1854 you can do a name search of the Catalogue. For those who were discharged between 1855 and 1872, the records are arranged alphabetically by name within regiment or corps. In order to trace a soldier's record for this period, it is necessary to know in which regiment or corps he served. From 1873 to 1882 the records are alphabetical by cavalry, artillery, infantry and corps, while from 1883 to 1913 they are alphabetical by surname for the whole Army. These records are currently being digitized to allow you to search by name of soldier. It is hoped that these will become available in 2009/10. First World War soldiers' service records may be found in WO 363 and WO 364. Both series are available on microfilm in the Open Reading Room and are free to download onsite at *www.ancestry.co.uk*.

9.4 Canal and Railway Companies

Another source for tracking ancestors who moved around the UK are canal and railway company records, particularly those records relating to the construction of lines on which many labourers were employed as navvies. The Railway Department of the Board of Trade was established in 1840; it assumed responsibility for canals in the 1850s. Board of Trade papers relating to canals can be found in BT 22 Railway

Department Correspondence and Papers, BT 13 Establishment Department Correspondence and Papers, BT 15 Finance Department Registered Files and BT 58 Companies Department Correspondence and Papers. The Board of Trade Railway Department records were inherited by the Ministry of Transport in 1919 and its correspondence and papers can be found in MT 6 and MT 11, and its minute books in MT 13. Although reference to individuals can be found in these papers, they are more likely to be papers relating to policy and the formation of many canal and railway companies.

Records of canal and railway companies themselves are to be found in the records formerly held at the British Transport Historical Records section (BTHR) which now form the RAIL, AN and some ZLIB and ZPER groups of records. Record series relating to particular canal companies are arranged alphabetically by company name and form the series RAIL 800–99, RAIL 1112, RAIL 1116–17, RAIL 1162–3 and RAIL 1168–71. Record series relating to individual railway companies are arranged alphabetically by company name and form the series RAIL 1–799 and RAIL 1175–88. Books and pamphlets on canals, railways and associated subjects are in the ZLIB series and periodicals in the ZPER series.

9.5 Seamen's Records

The main source for tracing details of merchant seamen and shipping, especially from the eighteenth century onwards, is the archives of the Registry of Shipping and Seamen (RSS). These records are held in a number of places. Some are with the RSS in Cardiff, some with the National Maritime Museum at Greenwich, some at the Memorial University of Newfoundland in Canada, some with the county record offices and National Archives of Scotland and Ireland. However, the bulk are held at the National Archives. Merchant seamen moved around the globe and the ships' musters from 1747 and agreements and crew lists from 1835 may be worth consulting. BT 98 Agreements and Crew Lists, Series I is arranged by port up to 1854 and then by ship's official number up to 1860. Unfortunately, only those for Dartmouth, Liverpool, Plymouth and Shields survive before 1800. Only some of the musters include crew names. The agreements and crew lists from 1835 provide valuable information such as town or country of birth and other details. Later records are in BT 99 Agreements and Crew Lists, Series II, but these are only a 10 per cent sample for each year, the vast majority being held at the Maritime History Archive of the Memorial University in Canada (*www.mun.ca/mha*). For a guide to these and other records of seamen, consult Records of *Merchant Shipping and Seamen* (1998).

Compulsory registration of merchant seamen began in 1835 with three series of registers of seamen and a register of seamen's 'tickets' to

1857. Of these the most useful to identify seamen are BT 114 Alphabetical Register of Seamen's Tickets and BT 113 Register of Seamen's Tickets, as they not only give places of birth but also a physical description of each man. Registration was discontinued after 1857 and only the Agreements and Crew Lists are available until the Central Index Register began in 1913. This is known as the Fourth Register of Seamen, and consisted of four large card indexes (BT 348–50 and BT 364). The Central Index was replaced by a Central Register of Seamen in 1941 and is sometimes known as the Fifth Register (BT 382 Fifth Register of Merchant Seamen's Service (CRS 10 forms) 1941–72). It is arranged in eight parts covering different ethnic groups. Parts One, 1941 to 1946, and Two, 1946 to 1972, cover mainly Europeans, but also include men of Afro-Caribbean descent.

BT 372 Central Register of Seamen: Seamen's Records ('Pouches'), includes records relating to individual seamen filed in an envelope 'pouch'. The contents of any particular pouch, however, may cover any period starting after 1913 and ending up to 1972 and possibly, although unlikely, beyond. When seamen were discharged, some or all of their documents (including the index cards) were placed in the

FIG. 43 *A list of employed West Africans in Liverpool in 1919 with biographical records.* HO 45/1101/377969

LIST OF EMPLOYED WEST AFRICANS. LIST. No. C

191

NAME. AGE. ADDRESS.	REMARKS.
(22) THOMAS WILLIAMS. 25 yrs. 2 Newton Street.	Born at Sierre Leone unmarried came here as a ship's fireman in 1900 joined the Navy in 1907 Discharged in June 1911, joined the Army 22/9/16 Discharged 7/8/18, rejoined the navy 9/9/18, still attached to the H.M.S. "Eaglet" now on demobilisation leave.
(23) TOBY DUITTE. 21 yrs. 42 St James Place.	Born at Sierre Leone, unmarried came to this country in 1916 as a ship's steward, now working on the S.S. "Roquelle" and expects to sail with her.
(24) JOSEPH ANOAH. 28 yrs. 2 Newton Street.	Born at Cape Coast Castle, unmarried came to this country in 1916 as a ship's steward, now working on the S.S.Chama" and expects to sail with her. joined the Cheshire Regt in August 1915 discharged in December 1916.
(25) PETER JOHNSON. 23 yrs. 2 Newton Street.	Born at Sierre Leone, unmarried came here in 1917 as a ship's fireman, has been working for the past 7 months as a dock labourer is awaiting £55 gratuity from the White Star Line re S.S."Justicia" torpedoed.
(26) JOE LEIGH. 29 yrs. 45 Beauford Street.	Born at Saboo unmarried came to this country 3 months ago as a ship's trimmer, now working on the S.S. "Roquelle" and expects to sail with her.
(27) JOHANNA DOUGLAS. 24 yrs 77 Hill Street.	Born at Bonny, unmarried came to this country in 1917 as a ship's fireman now employed as a labourer with George Jeager & Sons Burlington Street
(28) CHARLES BROWN. 24 yrs. 4 Hardy Street.	Born at Sierre Leone, unmarried came to this country in 1916 as a seaman now employed at Bibby's Oil Cake Mill.
(29) ISSAC MORGAN. 28 yrs. 4 Hardy Street.	Born at Cape Coast Castle unmarried came to this country in 1912 as a seaman, now working for the Leeds and Liverpool Canal Co.
(30) JIM DOE.25yrs 4 Hardy Street.	Born at Sierre Leone unmarried came to this country in 1913 as seaman now employed at Cattle Food Mills, Nailor Street.

pouches and these include discharges of seamen who were originally registered in the Central Index Register of 1913 to 1941. The pouches are arranged by discharge number within a number of series for different Commonwealth countries. They are searchable by name on the National Archives Online Catalogue. Full access to records in BT 372 and BT 382 is restricted. For those where the subjects are known to be dead or assumed dead (i.e. over 100 years) full access is granted; if not, the National Archives will supply a redacted copy omitting personal information such as national insurance numbers.

In the Home Office registered file series there is a record HO 45/11017/377969 relating to riots in Cardiff and Liverpool in 1919 involving West Indian and West African seamen. In sub-file 377969/44 are eight lists marked B to I, four of West Indians and four of West Africans, unemployed and employed, unmarried and married. The lists are quite detailed, giving name and address, age, country of birth and brief details of how each individual came to be in the United Kingdom. It was proposed to repatriate some of these men under the repatriation of coloured seamen schemes. There are 285 named, of which only some 59 were repatriated. The correspondence makes it clear that there had been several hundred black seamen in Liverpool at this time. Many had left the city, going to other towns inland.

9.6   Privy Council and Home Office Papers

Privy Council (PC) records contain papers relating to many different subjects. The most useful series PC 1 Miscellaneous Unbound Papers, for example, includes reports on the Irish in England and the meetings of the United Irishmen in London.

Home Office (HO) papers contain many documents relating to the Irish in Britain. Many of the matters relate to political gatherings and the meetings of Irish clubs in London and other parts of the country. Correspondence on disturbances, riots and political activities can be found in HO 40 Disturbances Correspondence 1812–55 and HO 41 Disturbances Entry Books. Most of the records in HO 41 contain a subject index. HO 45 Registered Correspondence and HO 144 Registered Correspondence, Supplementary contain general correspondence on a variety of domestic issues. These series may be searched by subject heading, the relevant headings being Ireland and Ireland (Fenians). HO 52 Counties Correspondence contains reports of local conditions, including riots, arson and other civil disturbances.

10 RESEARCH TECHNIQUES

Researching migrant ancestors can be complicated as there is no complete list of immigrants and emigrants for any period. There are some general rules though that can explain why you may not be able to find your migrant ancestors when you would expect to do so. Typical questions and useful solutions for family historians are outlined here for three major areas of research.

10.1 Passenger Lists

• I CAN'T FIND A CERTIFICATE OF ARRIVAL FOR MY ANCESTOR IN THE 1840S OR 1850S. The certificates of arrival in HO 2 and associated lists of alien passengers in HO 3 do not list all aliens. Exempt from certificates were children under the age of 14, and ambassadors and their accompanying staff. Also, increasingly the case in the 1840s during a relatively peaceful time in Europe, aliens were entering the UK unchecked, so neither appear in HO 2 or HO 3. In the minutes of evidence taken before the Select Committee on Laws affecting Aliens in 1843 (Parliamentary Papers reference 1843, volume V, p. 145), it was reported that no lists were provided by the masters at Liverpool in 1842 and there was no registration of aliens; at other ports the masters' lists showed that many aliens landed but failed to register. At London, 7,716 landed and 4,493 registered; at Dover, 1,277 landed and 1,237 registered; at Southampton, 1,197 landed and none registered; at Hull, 794 landed and one registered. In all, 11,600 aliens landed and 6,084 registered. In theory, the penalty for an alien failing to register was £2, and for a master failing to provide a list £20, but it appears that these fines were never exacted. The records were increasingly seen as being unreliable or incomplete and later returns were destroyed under statute.

• I CAN'T FIND AN ENTRY OF MY FATHER'S RETURN FROM ITALY IN THE INCOMING PASSENGER LISTS IN BT 26. BT 26 (as with BT 27) only records passengers on vessels that began or ended their journey in a British port or a port outside Europe and the Mediterranean area, so they do not include people travelling from or to Irish or European ports unless the final destination or point of embarkation was beyond Europe.

• I WAS EXPECTING TO FIND MORE INFORMATION ON BT 26 AND BT 27. Both BT 26 and BT 27 are fairly scant on detail. Until the First World War they record full name and occupation only (in addition to whether 'English', 'Scottish', 'Welsh', 'Irish' or 'Alien'). From 1914 an age field is introduced and from 1922 a field to record the address (in the UK). Inwards passenger lists held at other national archives are likely to include more detailed information, so always check these first. An increasing number are available online, including those for Canada and the United States. Plus, the majority pre-date the National Archives collection, which begins relatively late in 1890.

10.2 Records of Naturalization

• WHY CAN'T I FIND A RECORD OF NATURALIZATION? Make sure you search the Catalogue correctly. When you search by full name you must separate both names by the text AND, so Morris AND Muscovitz instead of Morris Muscovitz. Check that you're searching under the right name. Although some descriptions include aliases, others do not, so be sure to use an anglicized name as well as the original name where possible.

• STILL NOT THERE? Of the millions of migrants who settled in the UK, relatively few actually applied for British nationality. Before 1844 it was an exceptionally rare and very complex process which involved obtaining a private Act of Parliament by introducing a private bill into Parliament. The process was simplified in 1844 when the Home Secretary was empowered to grant naturalizations upon application, but even this only resulted in 70,000 naturalizations between 1844 and 1934, a small proportion of the millions of immigrants who had settled in this country during that time. The following information may help you understand why your ancestors were not naturalized:

Even though the process was simplified in 1844, it was still relatively expensive and at times would cost several hundred pounds if converted to today's money.

Naturalization granted full rights of a natural-born citizen–specifically this meant the right to hold public office and to own and inherit land. From 1844 applicants simply had to provide a reason why they wanted to become British. Ask yourself whether your ancestors would have wanted to be naturalized and why – were they businessmen, tradesmen, politicians or in the British services? If so, they may have applied for and been granted naturalization.

From 1847, regulations demanded that the application should be signed by at least four householders (increased to five in 1880) who should vouch for the respectability of the candidate. These needed to be British-born subjects who had personally known the applicants for at least five years. Would your ancestors readily know such people, likely to be middle class?

From 1870, you could only apply for naturalization if you had lived in the UK for at least five years. If your ancestor did not meet this requirement then they would not have been naturalized.

From 1873, the Metropolitan and local police constabularies checked memorials, and applications were rejected if they were deemed to be disrespectful. Had your alien ancestor any criminal connection, no matter how minor? This could have affected the decision of the Home Secretary.

• BUT IT SAYS HE WAS NATURALIZED IN THE CENSUS RETURNS. Information provided by householders to the census enumerators was rarely checked, including the nationality of individuals. As such, returns are riddled with inaccuracies. There is plenty of evidence to imply wrongly that people had been naturalized. Why this information was falsely given we don't fully know, but undoubtedly aliens may have felt intimidated by questions from strangers and felt more secure if they said that they were British when they were not.

• I HAVE A FEMALE ANCESTOR WHO I KNOW WAS DEFINITELY BRITISH, BUT IS NOT IN THE INDEX TO NATURALIZATIONS. In which case it is likely that she became British upon marriage. Before 1948, women would take the nationality of their spouse. So, if they were British-born but married a German immigrant, then they would become a German national. If they outlived their spouse or if they divorced, then they would need to reapply for British nationality. Similarly, alien women could become British upon marriage to a man of British nationality. Again, if he pre-deceased her or if they got a divorce, she would revert to her alien nationality and lose her British status. In either case, the Home Secretary would not need to get involved. There would be no application of certificate of naturalization issued. The proof of nationality would be on the marriage certificate. This policy explains why over 95 per cent of all naturalizations by the Secretary of State before 1948 relate to male applicants.

• I'VE FOUND AN ENTRY OF NATURALIZATION IN THE INDEX BUT THE PAPERS DON'T SURVIVE. When the name indexes to naturalizations were added to the National Archives catalogue in 2002 these created online access to the descriptions of some 70,000 naturalization case files between 1844 and 1935. The project identified misfiled papers but also revealed those papers where the papers have not survived – a very small proportion, a few hundred between 1844 and 1935. The original paper indexes in the Open Reading Room still list these missing papers and access to the certificates in HO 334 is still possible.

10.3   Internment

• I CAN'T FIND AN INTERNMENT RECORD FOR AN ANCESTOR ON THE MOVING HERE SITE. The downloaded internment tribunal cards from 1939 on the Moving Here site relate to those 'enemy' aliens who were not assessed for internment and at liberty in the UK. Cards where a decision was made to intern are not on Moving Here. These are only available at the National Archives on microfilm on HO 396 and there is no name index on the Catalogue for these records.

• ON THE INTERNMENT CARD THERE IS A HOME OFFICE REFERENCE – CAN I TAKE THIS FURTHER? Home Office papers for aliens assessed for internment are destined for the series HO 405 – many are at the National Archives already. Others (for surnames beginning with 'O' onwards) are in the custody of the Home Office.

• AND THERE IS A POLICE REGISTRATION NUMBER? This relates to alien registration cards first issued in 1914, the majority of which have been destroyed under statute. A small sample for London survive in MEPO 35. Those administered by other police forces are held locally at Police Museums or local record offices.

APPENDIX 1

A Chronology of Key Legislation

Before the eighteenth century, there was little general legislation regarding citizenship, and those laws that were passed tended to relate only to restrictions imposed on foreign merchants and craftsmen, or immigrants, whether denizens or naturalized. Nevertheless, the early legislation outlined below may still be considered important in helping to shape the general laws of nationality that emerged later. This list should not be considered comprehensive, but includes Acts available to consult in the Library collection of the National Archives (TNA).

1523   An Act (14 and 15 Hen. VIII c. 2) to regulate stranger craftsmen.

1529   An Act (21 Hen. VIII c. 16) to ratify a decree of Star Chamber requiring all aliens (including denizens) to swear allegiance to the king. This condition was, by an Act (7 Jas. I c. 2) in 1609, extended to include all naturalized aliens as a result of anti-Catholic feeling. The Act of 1529 was also designed to control craftsmen and regulate their relationship to the City livery companies.

1540   An Act (32 Hen. VIII c. 16) to strengthen the law relating to stranger denizens and patents of denization.

Between 1660 and 1710 a number of attempts were made to pass through Parliament a true naturalization bill, one that would apply to all aliens.

1701   The Act of Succession (12 and 13 Will. III. c. 2) provided, in clause 3, that no person born out of England, Scotland or Ireland although naturalized or made a denizen, should be capable of being of the Privy Council, of Parliament or of holding office or trust under the Crown or of having grants of land under the Crown.

1708   The Act for Naturalization of Foreign Protestants (7 Anne c. 5) made provision for the huge numbers of Huguenot refugees entering the country by providing a simpler method for naturalizing foreigners. When the tide of Huguenot refugees became a flood, the forms of denization procedure were relaxed and leave was granted by Order in Council for the wholesale grants of denizations without the payment of any fee. In passing the Act, Parliament recognized the opportunity for increasing wealth by simplifying the process of naturalization. The Act enabled aliens to be declared natives on taking the oaths of allegiance and signing the declaration in the Courts of England, Scotland or the Quarter Sessions. They also needed to produce proof that they had taken the Sacrament in some Protestant or reformed congregation within the United Kingdom in the past three months. The Act was repealed in 1710, apart from one clause which allowed for children born abroad of natural-born subjects to be taken to be natural-born subjects themselves.

In general, late eighteenth- and nineteenth-century naturalization legislation resulted in lightening the disabilities of naturalized aliens and simplifying and cheapening the forms of admission.

1731   By an Act (4 Geo. II c. 21) children whose fathers were or were to become naturalized British citizens would themselves be taken to be natural-born subjects. Previously, it was required that both father and mother had to have been natural-born subjects.

1773   By a further Act (13 Geo. III c. 21) the principle outlined above was extended to the children of the children affected by the 1731 Act.

1793   An Aliens Act (33 Geo. III c. 4) was passed by the government requiring aliens to register by means of declarations signed at ports of entry. A Superintendent of Aliens was appointed and an Aliens Office created. Further acts were passed in 1816 and 1826.

1836   The Aliens Act (6 and 7 Will. IV c. 11) led to a reorganization which incorporated the Aliens Office into the Home Office. It introduced some relaxation in the system of registration, but continued the requirement that masters of vessels and aliens should make a declaration on arrival.

1844   The Naturalization Act (7 and 8 Vict. c. 66) provided that every alien residing in Great Britain with intent to settle should present a memorial to the Secretary of State stating age, trade and duration of residence. Thereupon the Secretary of State would issue to the applicant a certificate granting rights of a natural-born subject with the exception of the right of being of the Privy Council or Parliament. The Act maintained the taking of the oath of allegiance and Act of Succession and provided that any woman married to a natural-born or naturalized person was deemed naturalized herself. It further stipulated that applicants wishing to become naturalized citizens should state their intention to reside and settle in Great Britain.

1870   The Naturalization Act (33 and 34 Vict. c. 14) laid down a qualification period so that applicants had to have resided in the United Kingdom or served the Crown for a period of at least five years before being eligible for consideration.

The First World War prompted a tightening of the legislation governing immigration. Apart from a brief move to more inclusive policy in the aftermath of the Second World War, this would be the pattern for the remainder of the century.

1905   The Aliens Act (5 Edw. VII c. 13) provided for a new system of immigration control and registration and placed responsibility for all matters of immigration and nationality on the Home Secretary.

1914   The Aliens Registration Act (4 and 5 Geo. V c. 12). As the name suggests, this Act made mandatory the registration with the police of all aliens over the age of 16.

Under the British Nationality and Status Act (4 and 5 Geo. V c. 17) the statutory qualification of applicants was extended to record that applicants must be of good character and must have an adequate knowledge of English.

1922   The British Nationality and Status of Aliens Act (12 and 13 Geo. V. ch. 44). This act allowed those born overseas to British parents to be registered as British subjects within one year of birth.

1948   The British Nationality Act 1948 (11 and 12 Geo. VI c. 56) made provision for different categories of certificates for the registration of British citizenship. This applied to British subjects or citizens of Ireland, the Channel Islands, Isle of Man, any colony, protectorate and certain protected states.

1962   The Commonwealth Immigrants Act (10 and 11 Eliz. II c. 21) required all Commonwealth citizens seeking employment in Britain to qualify for an employment voucher. This limited the right of entry to the United Kingdom; those with passports not issued in Britain were obliged to hold a work permit to secure entry.

1968   The Commonwealth Immigrants Act (1968 c. 9) further tightened controls. Potential immigrants were now required to prove that they themselves were born in the United Kingdom, or that their parents or grandparents had been.

The Immigration Act (1971 c. 77), came into force on 1 January 1973 and brought Commonwealth citizens into line with citizens of foreign countries in so far as employment was concerned. It required Commonwealth citizens to have prospective employers in order to come to the United Kingdom for employment. By order of this Act, nationals of countries within the European Union did not require work permits.

1981   The British Nationality Act (1981 c. 61) created five categories of citizenship: British Citizenship, British Dependent Territories Citizenship, British Overseas Citizenship, British Protected Person, and British Subject.

APPENDIX 2

Migration Records at the National Archives

Series	Description	Indexed by name online	Original	Microfilm	Online
HO 1	Naturalisation papers, 1801–71	on *The Catalogue*	X		
HO 144	Naturalisation papers, 1879–1934	on *The Catalogue*	X		
HO 382	Alien Files/Naturalisation papers (famous cases), 1934–48	on *The Catalogue*	X		
HO 405	Alien Files/Naturalisation papers, 1934–48	on *The Catalogue*	X		
HO 44	Denization Papers, 1789–1832	on *The Catalogue*	X		
HO 45	Naturalisation papers, 1872–8	on *The Catalogue*	X		
HO 334	Duplicate naturalisation certificates/registrations of British nationality, 1870–1987	on *The Catalogue* for years 1870-1934 only searching via HO 1, 44 and 334	X		
C 54	Enrolled copies of naturalisation certificates, 1844–73				
C 97	Letters Patent of Denization, 1752–1830	on *The Catalogue*			
RG 4	Includes baptisms, marriages and burial returns of foreign churches, 1567 and 1840	online at www.bmdregisters.co.uk			X
HO 2*	Aliens certificates of arrival, 1826–52	online at www.ancestry.co.uk			X
HO 3*	Alien passenger lists, 1836–69	online at www.ancestry.co.uk			X
HO 4	Patents of Denization		X		
HO 5*	Aliens entry books, 1794–1921	online at www.ancestry.co.uk			X
BT 26	Inwards Passenger Lists, 1878–1960	online at www.ancestry.co.uk			X
BT 27	Outwards Passenger Lists, 1890–1960	online at www.ancestorsonboard.com			X
FO 737	Passport applications, sample selection, 1916–83	on *The Catalogue*	X		
FO 655	Collection of passports issued, 1802–1961	on *The Catalogue*	X		
FO 610	Passport Registers, 1795–1948		X		
FO 611	Passport Registers Indexes of Names, 1851–1916			X	

Series	Description	Indexed by name online	Original	Microfilm	Online
AO 12	American Loyalists Claims, Series I, 1776–83		X		
AO 13	American Loyalists Claims, Series II, 1780–1835		X		
MH 12**	Poor Law Union Correspondence, 1833–1909		X		
BH 1	Hudson's Bay Company Archives, 1667–1900			X	
CO 384	Emigration Original Correspondence, 1817–96		X		
E 157	Registers of Licences to pass beyond the seas, 1573–1677		X		
HO 107 & RG 9-12	Decennial Census returns of England & Wales, 1841–91	online at www.ancestry.co.uk	X		
RG 13	1901 Census returns of England & Wales, 1901	online at www. 1901censusonline.com	X		
RG 14*	1911 Census Schedules of England & Wales, 1911	online at www.1911census.co.uk	X		
HO 47	Judges' Reports on Criminals, 1784–1829	on *The Catalogue*	X		
HO 11	Convict Transportation Registers, 1787–1870			X	
DO 131	Children's Overseas Reception Board, 1940–59	on *The Catalogue*	X		
MEPO 35	Sample Police Alien registration cards	on *The Catalogue* and *DocumentsOnline*	X (for cases under 100 years old)		X (for cases over 100 years old)
MH 8	Belgian Refugees: history cards, 1914–19		X		
HO 294	Czechoslovak Refugee family records, 1939–47	on *The Catalogue*	X		
HO 396/1 -106	Internee Tribunal cards (category A – at liberty), 1939–40	online at www.movinghere.org.uk			X
HO 396/ 107-308	Internee Tribunal cards (categories B and C – at liberty), 1939–47			X	
HO 215	Internees, Sample Personal Files, 1939–45	on *The Catalogue*	X		
HO 372	Registers of Deportees, 1906–63		X		
LAB 42	Commonwealth Immigrants: Application for Employment Vouchers, 1962–8	on *The Catalogue*	X		
LAB 48	Applications for Work Permits, 1968–75	on *The Catalogue*	X		

* expected from Spring 2009   ** for a limited number of Unions

FURTHER READING AND WEBSITES

The best general introduction to family history in the National Archives is Amanda Bevan's *Tracing Your Ancestors in the National Archives* (7th edition, TNA, 2006). The Office also produces a number of Research Guides. These are intended to be used at Kew in conjunction with the records. Please ask in the Open Reading Room. Alternatively, you can download them via the National Archives website.

A large number of websites are now available to those researching ancestors who came to or departed from Britain. However, Moving Here, which covers Jewish, Irish, Caribbean and South East Asian migration to England after 1800, remains one of the most useful. This website offers online versions of original material, including photographs, personal papers, government documents, maps and art objects, as well as a large collection of sound recordings and video clips.

Books

C.M. Andrews, *Guide to the Materials for American History to 1783 in the Public Record Office of Great Britain* (2 vols, Carnegie Institution, Washington, 1912 and 1914)

M.K. Banton, *Administering the Empire, 1801-1968: A Guide to the Records of the Colonial Office in the National Archives of the UK* (Institute of Historical Research, 2008)

I.A. Baxter, *Brief Guide to Bibliographical Sources in the India Office Library* (London, 1979; second edition 1990)

E. Bull, *Aided Immigration from Britain to South Africa, 1857–1867* (Pretoria, 1991)

E.M. Carus-Wilson ed., *The Overseas Trade of Bristol in the Later Middle Ages*, British Record Society (1937)

D. Chapman, *People of the First Fleet* (Cassell, 1981)

H.S. Cobb ed., *The Overseas Trade of London 1480–1* (London Record Society, 1990)

P.S. Coldham, *The Complete Book of Emigrants, 1607–1776* (4 vols, Baltimore, 1987–93)

D.G. Crawford, *Roll of the Indian Medical Service 1615–1930* (London, 1930)

D.M. Daren ed., *The Making of King's Lynn: A Documentary Survey* (British Academy, Records of Social and Economic History, IX, 1984)

P.G. Fidlon and R.J. Ryan eds., *1788: The First Fleeters* (Australian Documents Library, 1981)

P.W. Filby and M.K. Meyer eds., *Passenger and Immigration Lists Index* (Detroit, 1981 and annual supplements)

M. Flynn, *The Second Fleet: Britain's grim convict armada of 1790* (Library of Australian History, 1989)

J. Gibson, *Poor Law Union Records* (4 vols, Gibson Guides, 1993)

M. Gillen, *The Founders of Australia: A Biographical Dictionary of the First Fleet* (Library of Australian History, 1989)

D.P. Henige, *Colonial Governors from the fifteenth century to the present: a comprehensive list* (University of Wisconsin, Madison, 1970)

V.C.P. Hodson, *List of the Officers of the Bengal Army* (4 vols, London, 1927–47)

J.C. Hotten, *Original Lists of Persons Emigrating to America, 1600–1700* (London, 1874)

R. Kershaw and J. Sacks, *New Lives for Old: the Story of Britain's Child Migrants* (TNA, 2008)

J.M. Kitzmuller, *In Search of the 'Forlorn Hope': a Comprehensive Guide to Locating British Regiments and their Records* (Salt Lake City, 1988)

W. Page, *Letters of Denizen and Acts of Naturalization for Aliens in England, 1509–1603* (Huguenot Society, Lymington, 1893)

P. Philip, *British Residents at the Cape, 1795–1819* (Cape Town, 1981)

L.L. Robson, *The Convict Settlers of Australia* (Melbourne University Press, 1965)

R.J. Ryan, *The Third Fleeters* (Horwitz Grahame, 1983)

W.A. Shaw, *Letters of Denizen and Acts of Naturalization for Aliens in England, 1603–1800* (Huguenot Society, 1932)

A. Thurston, *Records of the Colonial Office, Dominions Office, Commonwealth Relations Office and Commonwealth Office* (HMSO, 1995)

Records of Merchant Shipping and Seamen (PRO Readers' Guide No. 20, 1998)

Websites

National Archives
www.nationalarchives.gov.uk
www.nas.gov.uk
www.nationalarchives.ie
www.collectionscanada.gc.ca
www.naa.gov.au
Ancestry and family history sites
www.movinghere.org.uk
www.jewishgen.org
www.agfhs.org.uk
www.anglo-italianfhs.org.uk
www.casbah.ac.uk
www.sog.org.uk
www.ffhs.org.uk
Passenger lists
www.ancestry.co.uk
www.immigrantsships.net
www.ellisisland.org
www.castlegarden.org
www.ancestorsonboard.com

INDEX